PENGUIN BOOKS

CHURCHILL: A Photographic Portrait

Martin Gilbert was born in London in 1936, and was educated at Highgate School. After two years National Service in the Army, he went to Magdalen College, Oxford, where he obtained a First Class Degree in Modern History. For two years he did research as a Senior Scholar at St Antony's College, Oxford, and he was then elected to a Fellowship at Merton College, Oxford, where he continued with his historical researches from 1962 to 1968, publishing several books, including a series of historical atlases. In 1962 he had joined Randolph Churchill's research team, collecting material for the official life of Sir Winston Churchill; and in 1968 he succeeded Randolph Churchill as Official Biographer, responsible for the period from 1914 until Churchill's death.

OTHER BOOKS BY
MARTIN GILBERT

WINSTON S. CHURCHILL, VOL III, 1914–1916
THE EUROPEAN POWERS 1900–1945
THE ROOTS OF APPEASEMENT
SIR HORACE RUMBOLD: PORTRAIT OF A DIPLOMAT
RECENT HISTORY ATLAS
BRITISH HISTORY ATLAS
AMERICAN HISTORY ATLAS
JEWISH HISTORY ATLAS
FIRST WORLD WAR ATLAS
RUSSIAN HISTORY ATLAS
THE APPEASERS (*with Richard Gott*)

Editions of documents

BRITAIN AND GERMANY BETWEEN THE WARS
PLOUGH MY OWN FURROW, THE LIFE OF LORD ALLEN OF HURTWOOD
SERVANT OF INDIA: THE VICEROY'S PRIVATE SECRETARY 1905–1910
CHURCHILL (*Spectrum Books*)
LLOYD GEORGE (*Spectrum Books*)

For young readers

WINSTON CHURCHILL (*Clarendon Biography*)
WINSTON CHURCHILL (*Jackdaw*)
THE COMING OF WAR IN 1939 (*Jackdaw*)
THE SECOND WORLD WAR

Editor

A CENTURY OF CONFLICT: ESSAYS FOR A. J. P. TAYLOR

CHURCHILL:

A PHOTOGRAPHIC PORTRAIT

BY

MARTIN GILBERT

PENGUIN BOOKS
in association with William Heinemann

Penguin Books Ltd, Harmondsworth, Middlesex, England
Penguin Books Australia Ltd, Ringwood, Victoria, Australia
Penguin Books Canada Ltd, 41 Steelcase Road West, Markham, Ontario, Canada
First published 1974
Copyright © Martin Gilbert, 1974
Made and printed in Great Britain by
Butler & Tanner Ltd, Frome and London
Set in Times New Roman

Paperback SBN 14 00.3769 1
Hardback SBN 434 29196 X

Preface

My aim in these pages has been to portray, in a single photographic volume, something of the variety and span of Churchill's life; to show him in many different moods, and on many divers occasions. Although not all the major incidents of Churchill's long career were recorded in photographs, or even drawn by cartoonists, it is still possible to present, in visual form, a surprisingly large number of specific events from all periods of his life.

Although Churchill was much photographed, many of the original negatives have been destroyed, and many of the prints lost, since 1900. The natural ravages of time, the man-made processes of clearing-up and 'weeding out', the accident of fire, and the fierce destruction of the Blitz, have combined to eliminate for all time many important Churchill photographs. This process of destruction continues. During the course of my researches, a senior assistant in a leading photographic agency remarked: 'Periodically we go through destroying things. We do it every week. We haven't the space for them. We destroy precious, irreplaceable things.' Such destruction is commonplace, and, in view of the fact that negatives can easily be stored in university archives, it is also unnecessary. Much of the material lost by the current, continuing destruction is lost forever. Nevertheless, the number of surviving photographs is substantial, providing adequate scope for any single-volume selection.

Nearly half of the photographs in this volume come from Churchill's personal photograph albums. I have supplemented this important source with photographs from the Churchill papers, from the albums of his contemporaries, from institutions, and from several news agency archives. In November 1968, when I began to assemble this material, I appealed for photographs in over forty national and local newspapers. As a result of the ready response, I obtained much extra material, and the final selection of 364 photographs and cartoons was made from a total collection of over 5,000—sufficient to make at least another twelve volumes.

Throughout his political life, and particularly before 1940, Churchill was a popular subject for cartoonists; it was often their portrayal of him that lodged in the public mind. I have taken most of the cartoons from his own voluminous press cutting albums, which also contain several original photographs. On most pages I have tried to provide a quotation relevant to the illustrations, or to their themes. Most of these quotations come from material in the Churchill papers; some from the archives of his contemporaries; some from his speeches, and some from his books. I have listed the sources, both for the photographs and for the quotations, at the end of the volume.

I am particularly grateful to Baroness Spencer-Churchill, who allowed me to borrow her own photograph album, and to talk to her about the photographs. I am also grateful to Winston S. Churchill MP, Sir Winston Churchill's grandson, for putting his grandfather's photograph albums and press cutting books at my disposal.

In the early stages of my research I was greatly helped and encouraged by the late Field Marshal Earl Alexander of Tunis, and by Field Marshal Viscount Montgomery of Alamein, both of whom let me use their extensive photograph collections, and answered my many questions about the events portrayed in them. I am also extremely grateful to those individuals who provided photographs which I have used in this volume, or who gave me information which enabled me to trace photographs. In particular I should like to thank J. R. A. Bailey; Therize Borry; A. Butterworth; Peregrine S. Churchill; John Davie; John Freeman; D. Freeman; Major-General Sir Edmund Hakewill Smith; Miss Grace Hamblin; James Harvey; Lady Patricia Kingsbury; Mrs Constance Mainprice; A. Massen; Paul Maze; J. J. Moss; Mr Rance; Sir Geoffrey Shakespeare; Harry Skinner; Mr and Mrs H. Sornsen; the 2nd Viscount Trenchard; Dr J. Van Roey; Ava, Viscountess Waverley; and Peter Woodard.

Nearly two-thirds of the photographs in this volume are from private sources. But the book could not have been completed without the help of those news agencies in whose care are many of the most important photographs, often in the form of glass plate negatives. The following news agencies, institutions, and archives provided material: Acme News Pictures; Associated Newspapers; Barratts Photo Press; Bassano & Vandyk; Camera Press; The Cardiff Naturalists Society; Central Press Photos; The Czechoslovak Army Film & Photo Service; The Daily Mirror Picture Service; European Picture Service; Fox Photos; Paris Match; The Press Association; The Radio Times Hulton Picture Library; The Imperial War Museum; The London News Agency; The Sport and General Press Agency; Syndication International; Thomson Newspapers; Time Incorporated; Topical Press Agency; and United Press International.

The selection of the photographs, the cartoons and the quotations is my own. But I am grateful to Miss Susie Sacher, who advised me on the selection, the layout and the cover; to Mrs Charmian Allam, who did all the typing; and to Miss Mary Tyerman, who provided detailed information about several of the incidents portrayed in the photographs. My particular thanks are due to Jerry Moeran, of Studio Edmark, Oxford, and to his assistant Miss Jean Hunt, who prepared many of the prints used for this volume from faded or damaged originals, and who copied all the cartoons from the original press cuttings.

It has not always been possible to give the precise date of a particular photograph, or to identify all the people in it. I would be extremely grateful to any reader who can provide more precise dating, or any further identification. I should also welcome new photographs for use in future editions, or in the remaining volumes of the official biography.

Merton College
Oxford
29 August 1973

MARTIN GILBERT

CHURCHILL: A Photographic Portrait

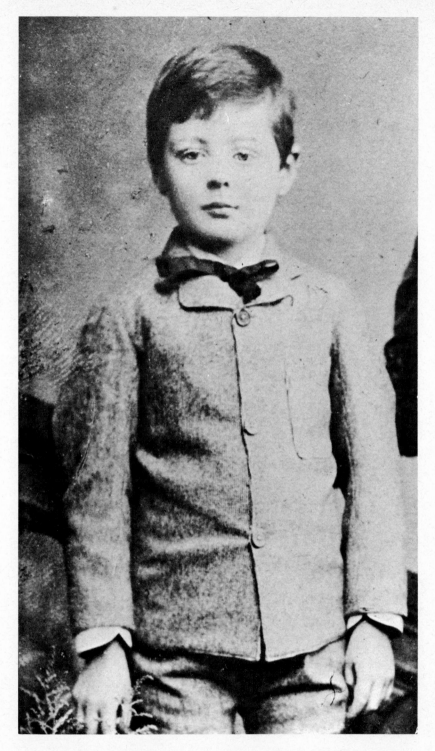

1 Winston Leonard Spencer Churchill was born on 30 November 1874, at Blenheim Palace. This photograph was taken in Dublin, when Churchill was five.

2 Churchill's mother, Lady Randolph Churchill, an American by birth. In 1874, when her son Winston was born, she was twenty years old. A central figure in fashionable society, she saw little of her son during his childhood. In his memoirs, published in 1930, Churchill wrote: *'She shone for me like the Evening Star. I loved her dearly – but at a distance.'*

3 Churchill in 1881, in his sailor suit. Throughout his childhood he was fascinated by armies and fleets. On 4 January 1882 he wrote to his mother from Blenheim Palace: '*I thank you very much for those beautiful presents those Soldiers and Flags and Castle they are so nice....*' On 1 April 1882 he wrote again: '*I have been playing out of doors at making encampments which is great fun. I pretend to pitch a tent and make the umbrella do for it.*' On 6 February 1883 he wrote: '*I am longing for another feudal castle.*'

4 Churchill's father, Lord Randolph Churchill; a photograph taken in about 1884 when Lord Randolph was thirty-five. In 1885, while his father was in India, Churchill wrote to him: '*When are you coming home again. I hope it will not be long. I am at school now and am getting on pretty well. Will you write and tell me about India what it's like. It must be very nice and warm out there now, while we are so cold in England. Will you go out on a tiger Hunt while you are there? Are the Indians very funny? . . . Try and get me a few stamps for my stamp album, Papa. Are there many ants in India if so, you will have a nice time, what with ants mosquitos. Every body wants to get your signature will you send me a few to give away? I am longing to see you so much.*' In 1885 Lord Randolph had become Secretary of State for India; in the following year he was made Chancellor of the Exchequer and Leader of the House of Commons. Although young, he was one of the most popular and forceful speakers of his time, and seen by many as a future Conservative Prime Minister.

6 Lady Randolph Churchill with her two sons, Jack and Winston; a photograph taken in 1889, when Jack was nine and Winston fourteen. On 1 January 1891, Churchill wrote to his mother from Banstead Manor, near Newmarket, where he and his brother were on holiday together: '*We have slaughtered many rabbits – About 11 brace altogether. Tomorrow we slay the rats. The Pond is frozen 8 inches – The ground is covered with 4 inches of snow. Pipes are frozen – Oil freezes in the kitchen. No wind. V-happy. V. well. We are enjoying ourselves very much. We exist on onions and Rabbits & other good things.*' Jack, who became stockbroker, died in 1947.

5 Mrs Everest, Churchill's nurse from 1875. In his memoirs Churchill wrote: '*Mrs Everest it was who looked after me and tended all my wants. It was to her I poured out my many troubles . . .*' On 29 July 1888, when he was thirteen, Churchill wrote to his mother, from Harrow School: '*Could you let Everest come down, bring my clothes. . . . Do let Everest come, because my ideas of packing are very limited. . . . If you will let Everest come please telegraph by what train she will arrive or I shall not know what to do.*'

7 Churchill as a schoolboy; a photograph probably taken in 1889. His school reports caused his parents continual anxiety. On 12 June 1890 his mother wrote to him: '. . . *your work is an insult to your intelligence. If you would only trace out a plan of action for yourself & carry it out & be determined to do so – I am sure you could accomplish anything you wished. It is that thoughtlessness of yours which is your greatest enemy.*'

8

Lord Randolph Churchill in 1893, the year before his death at the age of forty-five, and the year in which his son succeeded in entering Sandhurst. On hearing the news of his son's success, Lord Randolph, who was already very ill, wrote to him, on 9 August 1893: *'There are two ways of winning in an examination, one creditable the other the reverse. You have unfortunately chosen the latter method, and appear to be much pleased with your success. The first extremely discreditable feature of your performance was missing the infantry, for in that failure is demonstrated beyond refutation your slovenly happy-go-lucky harum scarum style of work for which you have always been distinguished at your different schools. . . . With all the advantages you had, with all the abilities which you foolishly think yourself to possess & which some of your relations claim for you, with all the efforts that have been made to make your life easy & agreeable & your work neither oppressive or distasteful, this is the grand result that you come up among the 2nd rate & 3rd rate class who are only good for commissions in a cavalry regiment. . . . I am certain that if you cannot prevent yourself from leading the idle useless unprofitable life you have had during your schooldays & later months, you will become a mere social wastrel one of the hundreds of the public school failures, and you will degenerate into a shabby unhappy & futile existence. If that is so you will have to bear all the blame for such misfortunes yourself.'*

9 Churchill with two fellow officer-cadets at the Royal Military College, Sandhurst. On 3 September 1893, after three days as a cadet, he wrote to his father: '*The Discipline is extremely strict – Far stricter than Harrow. Hardly any law is given to juniors on joining. No excuse is ever taken – not even with a plea of "didn't know" after the first few hours: and of course no such thing as unpunctuality or untidiness is tolerated. Still there is something very exhilarating in the military manner in which everything works; and I think that I shall like my life here during the next 18 months very much.*' Later in his letter Churchill wrote: '*The dinner is very grand – and the names of the dishes are written in French on the menu. There is nothing else French about them.*'

10 Churchill in fancy dress at Sandhurst, 11 May 1894. Two days earlier he had written to his mother: '*Please try to get me a costume and send it by the guard of the train at 11.45. I will meet it. Try to get a gorrilla or something amusing.*'

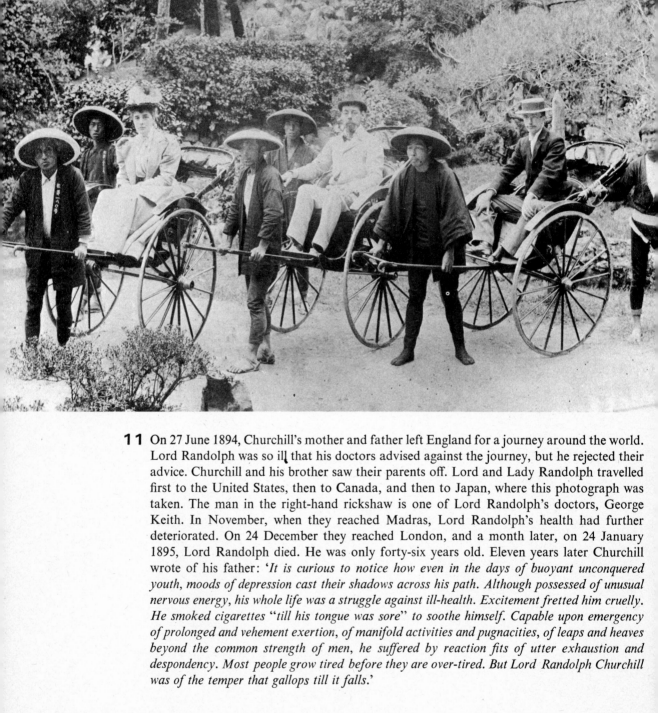

11 On 27 June 1894, Churchill's mother and father left England for a journey around the world. Lord Randolph was so ill that his doctors advised against the journey, but he rejected their advice. Churchill and his brother saw their parents off. Lord and Lady Randolph travelled first to the United States, then to Canada, and then to Japan, where this photograph was taken. The man in the right-hand rickshaw is one of Lord Randolph's doctors, George Keith. In November, when they reached Madras, Lord Randolph's health had further deteriorated. On 24 December they reached London, and a month later, on 24 January 1895, Lord Randolph died. He was only forty-six years old. Eleven years later Churchill wrote of his father: '*It is curious to notice how even in the days of buoyant unconquered youth, moods of depression cast their shadows across his path. Although possessed of unusual nervous energy, his whole life was a struggle against ill-health. Excitement fretted him cruelly. He smoked cigarettes "till his tongue was sore" to soothe himself. Capable upon emergency of prolonged and vehement exertion, of manifold activities and pugnacities, of leaps and heaves beyond the common strength of men, he suffered by reaction fits of utter exhaustion and despondency. Most people grow tired before they are over-tired. But Lord Randolph Churchill was of the temper that gallops till it falls.*'

12 Churchill and his mother; a photograph taken shortly after Lord Randolph's death, when Churchill himself was only twenty years old. Three years later in 1898, he wrote in his book 'The River War', of the Mahdi: '*Solitary trees, if they grow at all, grow strong; and a boy deprived of a father's care often develops, if he escapes the perils of youth, an independence and vigour of thought which may restore in after life the heavy loss of early days.*'

14 On 11 September 1896 Churchill sailed with the Fourth Hussars to India, reaching Bombay on 2 October. He remained in India for nearly two years, during which time he was in action on the North-West Frontier. On several occasions, in the midst of battle, he was nearly killed. On 19 September 1897 he wrote to his mother: '*I rode on my grey pony all along the skirmish line where everyone else was lying down in cover. Foolish perhaps but I play for high stakes and given an audience there is no act too daring or too noble. Without the gallery things are different. I will write again soon if all goes well, if not you know my life has been a pleasant one, quality not quantity is after all what we should strive for. Still I should like to come back and wear my medals at some big dinner or some other function.*'

13 A month before his father's death Churchill had taken the final Sandhurst examination. He passed it, coming 20th in the list of 130 candidates. His best marks were for Tactics, Fortifications and Riding. On 19 February 1895 he joined the Fourth Hussars at Aldershot, and on the following day was Gazetted a 2nd Lieutenant. His pay was £120 a year. Even during his first year as a soldier, his thoughts were on politics. On 16 August 1895 he wrote to his mother: '*It is a fine game to play – the game of politics – and it is well worth waiting for a good hand before really plunging. At any rate – four years of healthy and pleasant existence, combined with both responsibility & discipline can do no harm to me – but rather good. The more I see of soldiering the more I like it, but the more I feel convinced that it is not my métier. Well, we shall see – my dearest Mamma.*'

15

At the beginning of 1898 Churchill pleaded with his mother to use her influence to help him to join Lord Kitchener's expedition for the reconquest of the Sudan. '*It is a pushing age*', he wrote to his mother on 10 January, '*and we must shove with the best.*' On 14 March, when he was twenty-five, he published an account of the war on the Indian frontier, entitled 'The Malakand Field Force'. In July the War Office attached him as a Lieutenant to the 21st Lancers. On 2 August he was in Cairo, where this photograph was taken. A month later, on 2 September, he took part in the cavalry charge of the 21st Lancers at the battle of Omdurman, writing to his mother two days after the battle: '*I was under fire all day and rode through the charge. You know my luck in these things. I was about the only officer whose clothes, saddlery, or horse were uninjured. I fired 10 shots with my pistol – all necessary – and just got to the end of it as we cleared the crush. I never felt the slightest nervousness and felt as cool as I do now. I pulled up and reloaded within 30 yards of their mass and then trotted after my troop who were then about 100 yards away. I am sorry to say I shot 5 men for certain and two doubtful. . . . Nothing touched me. I destroyed those who molested me and so passed out without any disturbance of body or mind.*'

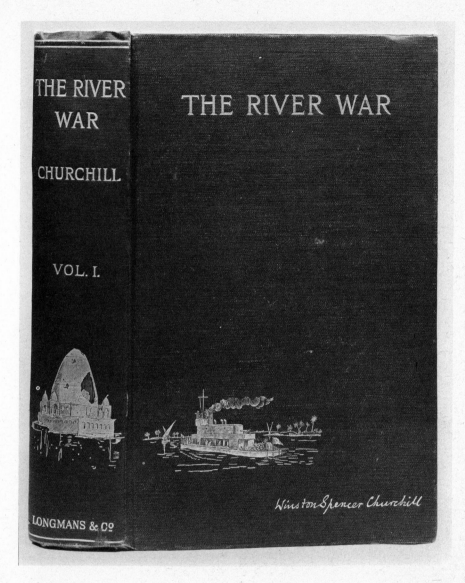

16 Immediately after the battle of Omdurman, Churchill began to write an account of the whole Sudan campaign. '*I work all day & every day at the book . . .*' he wrote to his mother on 21 December 1898. '*My hand gets so cramped. I am writing every word twice & some parts three times. It ought to be good since it is the best I can do.*' Entitled 'The River War', Churchill's book (his second) was published in England on 6 November 1899, and in the United States a month later.

18 Within four months of Churchill's defeat at Oldham, war broke out in South Africa between the British and the Boers. Churchill arranged to go to South Africa as war correspondent of the 'Morning Post'. He was paid £250 a month, a sum believed to be the highest ever paid up till then for a journalistic assignment. On 31 October 1899, he reached Cape Town. On 3 November he wrote to his mother: *'a fierce and bloody struggle is before us in which at least ten or twelve thousand lives will be sacrificed. . . .'* He himself was on his way to the scene of action, telling his mother: *'I shall believe I am to be preserved for future things.'*

17 Determined to enter politics, Churchill resigned his commission on 3 May 1899 after only four years in the Army. On 20 June he was adopted as Conservative candidate for Oldham. In his election address, dated 24 June, he declared: *'I regard the improvement of the condition of the British people as the main end of modern government.'* On 2 July he wrote to his friend Pamela Plowden about the election campaign: *'. . . it has been a strange experience and I shall never forget the succession of great halls packed with excited people until there was not room for a single person more – speech after speech, meeting after meeting – three even four in one night – intermittent flashes of Heat & Light & enthusiasm – with cold air and the rattle of a carriage in between: a great experience. And I improve every time – I have hardly repeated my-self at all. And at each meeting I am conscious of growing powers and facilities of speech. . . .'* The result was declared on 6 July; Churchill had been defeated, the Liberals victorious.

19 On 15 November 1899, at the invitation of Captain Aylmer Haldane, Churchill travelled by armoured-train on a reconnaissance through Boer-held territory. The train was derailed by the Boers, and Churchill, although only a war correspondent, at once offered Haldane his services. In his official report of the ambush Haldane wrote: '*For an hour efforts to clear the line were unsuccessful, as the trucks were heavy and jammed together, and the break-down gang could not be found, but Mr Churchill with indomitable perseverance continued his difficult task. . . . I would point out that while engaged on the work of saving the engine, for which he was mainly responsible, he was frequently exposed to the full fire of the enemy. I cannot speak too highly of his gallant conduct.*' The engine escaped; but Churchill, Haldane, and fifty others were captured. This photograph shows the derailed wagons on the day after the ambush.

20

Churchill's part in the armoured-train ambush was widely reported. This artist's drawing was published in the 'Saturday Herald' on 18 November 1899, only three days after the ambush. Its caption read: '*Young Churchill, a newspaper correspondent, at the battle of the armoured train, was obliged to seize a rifle and give the demoralised English soldiers a brave example. "Can't ye stand like men!" was his scornful cry.*'

"CAN'T YE STAND LIKE MEN!"

Arrivée à Pretoria des prisonniers du train blindé d'Estcourt (Lord Churchill à gauche en casquette).

La Guerre Anglo-Boer

Ed. Nels, Bruxelles. Serie Transvaal III

22 A Belgian postcard, showing the arrival of the armoured-train prisoners at Pretoria. Churchill is standing by the edge of the platform, wearing a flat cap. On 18 November 1899, three days after his capture, Churchill wrote to his mother from the State Model School, in which the prisoners were confined: '*Dearest Mamma, A line to explain that I was captured in the armoured train at Frere on the 15th, with some 50 officers and soldiers and some other non-combatants and platelayers and such like. As I was quite unarmed and in possession of my full credentials as a Press correspondent, I do not imagine they will keep me. . . . You need not be anxious in any way but I trust you will do all in your power to procure my release. After all this is a new experience – as was the heavy shell fire.*'

21 This artist's reconstruction of the armoured-train ambush was published in the 'Daily News Weekly' on 25 November 1899. The caption read: '*All the survivors praise Mr Winston Churchill's heroic conduct. He called for volunteers to help detach one of the wrecked trucks from the engine, and worked with them under the fire of three guns. When the wreckage was cleared the engine driver, who was wounded in the head, began to retire, but Mr Churchill called to him to come back, saying, "A man is never hit twice." The man brought back the engine, and Mr Churchill then helped to carry the wounded to the tender, and accompanied them back to Frere. There he jumped down with a rifle, and ran towards the enemy.*'

23 Churchill in captivity; Pretoria, 18 November 1899. He at once asked the Boers to release him, as he was a journalist and not a soldier, but the Boers refused. Of his time in prison he later wrote, in 'My Early Life': '*I certainly hated every minute of my captivity more than I have ever hated any other period in my whole life. . . . Looking back on those days, I have always felt the keenest pity for prisoners and captives.*' On 12 December 1899 Churchill, Haldane and Sergeant Major Brockie tried to escape over the wall of the prison; only Churchill succeeded in getting away. A Boer official in Pretoria offered a reward of £25 '*to anyone who brings the escaped prisoner of war Churchill dead or alive to this office*'. But Churchill managed to leave Boer territory, first on foot and then by train, undetected.

24

The news of Churchill's escape caused an even greater sensation than his capture had done. On 1 January 1900 an artist in the 'Illustrated Police News' gave his impression of the escape, and of Churchill's subsequent journey to the coast.

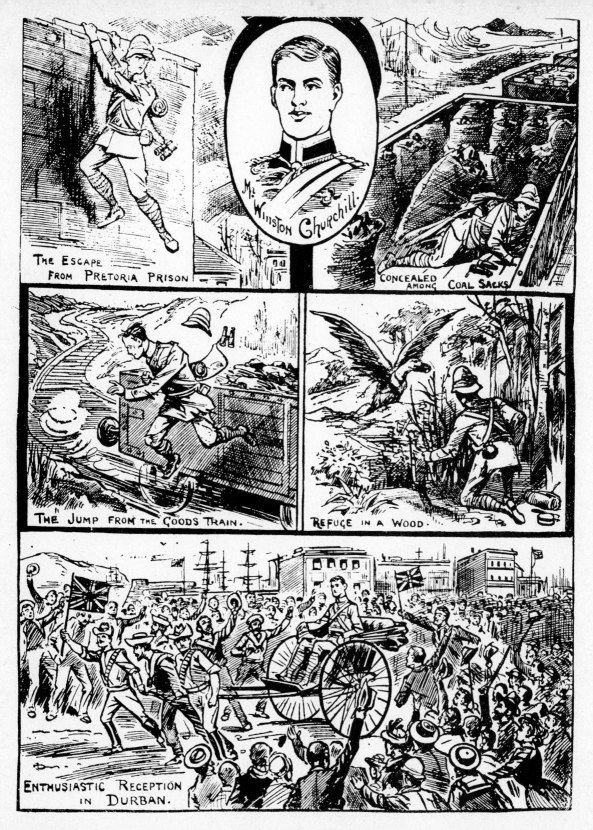

THE ESCAPE FROM PRETORIA PRISON

Mr. Winston Churchill

CONCEALED AMONG COAL SACKS

THE JUMP FROM THE GOODS TRAIN.

REFUGE IN A WOOD.

ENTHUSIASTIC RECEPTION IN DURBAN.

THE ESCAPE OF BRAVE WINSTON CHURCHILL FROM PRETORIA.

SIXTY HOURS OF TERRIBLE ANXIETY AND DARING ADVENTURES

26 General Buller's headquarters were only a few miles from the scene of the armoured-train ambush. Having rejoined the army, as a Lieutenant in the South African Light Horse, Churchill revisited the scene of his capture, which had just come under British control. On 6 January 1900 he wrote to his mother: '*There is a great battle – the greatest yet fought – impending here. And of course, I cannot run the risk of missing it. . . . These are anxious days, but when one is quite sure that one is filling ones proper place in the scheme of the world affairs, we may await events with entire composure. I should never care to go home to England, unless we are victorious here.*'

25 Churchill reached Durban on 23 December 1899, where he described his escape to an enthusiastic crowd. On the following day he set out for General Buller's headquarters, having decided to rejoin the army once more. On 26 December, General Buller wrote to Lady Londonderry: '*Winston Churchill turned up here yesterday escaped from Pretoria. He really is a fine fellow and I must say I admire him greatly. I wish he was leading irregular troops instead of writing for a rotten paper. We are very short of good men, as he appears to be, out here. . . .*'

27 A photograph of Churchill while he was a Lieutenant in the South African Light Horse (during the brief period when he tried to grow a moustache). In January he took part in the battle of Spion Kop, writing to Pamela Plowden on 28 January: '*For good or ill I am committed and I am content. I do not know whether I shall see the end or not, but I am quite certain that I will not leave Africa until the matter is settled. I should forfeit my self respect forever if I tried to shield myself like that behind an easily obtained reputation for courage. No possible advantage politically could compensate – besides believe me none would result. My place is here: here I stay – perhaps forever.*' And he added: '*The scenes on Spion Kop were among the strangest and most terrible I have ever witnessed.*'

28 In his letter to Pamela Plowden on 28 January Churchill wrote: '*I had five very dangerous days – continually under shell & rifle fire and once the feather in my hat was cut through by a bullet. But – in the end I came serenely through.*' And on 25 February he wrote to her: '*I was vy nearly killed two hours ago by a shrapnel. But though I was in the full burst of it God preserved me. Eight men were wounded by it. I wonder whether we shall get through and whether I shall live to see the end. There is a continual stream of wounded flowing by here to the hospitals – nearly a thousand in the last two days and five hundred before. The war is vy bitter but I trust we shall not show ourselves less determined than the enemy. My nerves were never better and I think I care less for bullets every day.*'

30 General Buller had allowed Churchill to remain a war correspondent as well as a soldier. Not only did he fight in the battles of 1900, but he also reported on them for the 'Morning Post'. This photograph shows sixteen of the war correspondents who covered the war. Immediately above Churchill is his friend J. B. Atkins, of the 'Manchester Guardian'; on Churchill's right, Basil Gotto of the 'Daily Express', on his left, F. W. Walker, also of the 'Daily Express'. In the front row are W. B. Wollin of the 'Sphere' (with pipe), J. O. Knight of the Chicago 'Times and Herald', and Ernest Prater of the 'Sphere'.

29 On 28 January 1900 Churchill's mother reached Durban on the hospital ship 'Maine', which had been purchased for £40,000 by a group of Anglo-Americans. Earlier, on 6 January, Churchill had written to her: '*I am so glad & proud to think of your enterprise & energy in coming out to manage the "Maine". Your name will long be remembered with affection by many poor broken creatures.*' One of Lady Randolph's first patients was her son Jack, for whom Churchill had secured a commission in the South African Light Horse, and who was wounded on 12 February 1900. '*He is unhappy at being taken off the board so early in the game*', Churchill wrote to his mother on 13 February. In this photograph, Jack poses with his mother on board the 'Maine'.

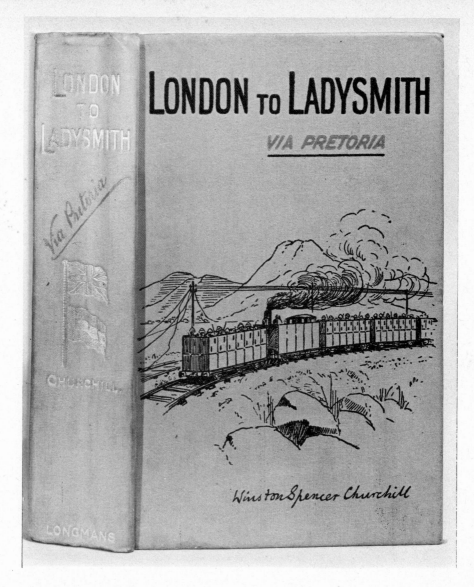

31 On 15 May 1900, while Churchill was still on active service in South Africa, a volume of his war despatches was published in London, entitled 'London to Ladysmith via Pretoria'. The book earned him more than £2,000. On the day of publication he wrote to his aunt Mrs Jack Leslie: '*I have had so many adventures that I shall be glad of a little peace and security. I have been under fire now in forty separate affairs, in this country alone and one cannnot help wondering how long good luck will hold. But I stand the wear and tear pretty well and indeed my health, nerve and spirits were never better than now at the end of seven months war.*'

32 Churchill sailed from Cape Town on 7 July 1900, reaching England on 20 July. His political ambitions were well understood by his contemporaries. This drawing by Spy was published in 'Vanity Fair' on 10 July, while he was still on his way home. The caption read: '*He is a clever fellow who has the courage of his opinions . . . He can write and he can fight, . . . he has hankered after Politics since he was a small boy, and it is probable that his every effort, military or literary, has been made with political bent . . . He is something of a sportsman; who prides himself on being practical rather than a dandy; he is ambitious; he means to get on, and he loves his country. But he can hardly be the slave of any Party.*'

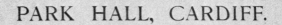

PARK HALL, CARDIFF.

The Committee of the Cardiff Naturalists Society beg to announce that Mr.

Winston Churchill, M.P.

Will give his deeply interesting Lecture, entitled :

"THE WAR AS I SAW IT"

ON

THURSDAY EVENING, NOVEMBER 29th, 1900, at 8.

The Lecture will be illustrated by Lantern Slides from Photos.

Mr. J. J. NEALE (*President of the Cardiff Naturalists Society*), will preside.

Doors open at 7.30.   Lecture at 8.   Carriages at 9.45.

RESERVED SEATS—Balcony, Front Row, 7/6; |Other Seats in Balcony, 5/-; Area, 3/6; UNRESERVED SEATS, 2/-.

Plan of the Hall may be seen and Tickets obtained at Mr. WM. LEWIS'S, Duke Street.

34 As soon as he had become a Member of Parliament, Churchill began a series of lectures on the South African War, both in England, where he earned £3,782 in 35 days, and in the United States, where he earned an average of £50 a night for over 30 nights. During 1899 and 1900 he had earned a total of £10,000 by his books, his journalism and his lectures.

33 On 25 July 1900, five days after reaching England from South Africa, Churchill was again adopted as Conservative candidate for Oldham. On 31 July he wrote to his brother Jack: '*I went to the House of Commons yesterday where I was treated with great civility by many people. . . . I have greatly improved my position in England by the events of last year. . . . The newspapers all give me paragraphs wherever I make a speech and a great many of the country newspapers write leading articles upon it.*' Churchill was elected to Parliament on 1 October 1900, two months before his twenty-sixth birthday.

35 Churchill as Conservative MP for Oldham. His first Parliamentary speeches were an attack on his own Party's proposal to increase British military expenditure. On 13 May 1901 he told the House of Commons: '*I have frequently been astonished since I have been in this House to hear with what composure and how glibly Members and even Ministers, talk of a European war . . . a European war can only end in the ruin of the vanquished and the scarcely less fatal commercial dislocation and exhaustion of the conquerors.*'

36

A cartoon in 'Punch', by E. T. Reed, published on 10 September 1902. Throughout 1902 Churchill continued to be dissatisfied with Conservative policies. In January, after reading Seebohm Rowntree's book 'Poverty: A Study of Town Life', he noted privately that '*this festering life at home makes world-wide power a mockery*'. In Parliament he advocated a generous peace with the Boers. On 10 October 1902 he described to Lord Rosebery his ideal of a Middle Party '*free at once from the sordid selfishness & callousness of Toryism on the one hand & the blind appetites of the Radical masses on the other*'.

"Yes, men of Oldham."

"It never got over my escape."

"The duties of confidential adviser
to Lord Roberts are not light."

"That's how I fetch Oldham."

38 Churchill with two friends, Henry Wilson (later Field Marshal Sir Henry Wilson) and, in the wheelchair, Auberon Herbert (later Lord Lucas). Herbert, who had lost a leg in the South African war, was killed in action while flying behind the German lines on 4 November 1916; Wilson was shot dead in London by two Sinn Fein assassins on 22 June 1922.

37 Churchill at Blenheim with the Duchess of Marlborough, formerly Consuelo Vanderbilt. During 1903 and 1904 he often stayed at Blenheim, writing a biography of his father. The book, entitled 'Lord Randolph Churchill', was published in two volumes on 2 January 1906. The publishers paid Churchill £8,000 for it. In it Churchill wrote of '*an England of wise men who gaze without self-deception at the failings and follies of both political parties, of brave and earnest men who find in neither faction fair scope for the effort that is in them*'.

39 A photograph of Churchill in 1904, taken after he had joined the Liberal Party. On 24 October 1903 he wrote to his friend Lord Hugh Cecil: '*I am an English Liberal. I hate the Tory party, their men, their words & their methods. I feel no sort of sympathy with them. . . .*' On 31 May 1904 he crossed the floor of the House of Commons to become a Liberal. During 1904 and 1905, he spoke throughout Britain, championing Free Trade, and denouncing the Conservatives. On 13 May 1905 he told a Manchester audience that the Conservative Party was '*a party of great vested interests, banded together in a formidable confederation, corruption at home, aggression abroad . . . dear food for the million, cheap labour for the millionaire*'.

HESITATING.

"Mr. Winston Churchill's inclusion in the Liberal party, though not formally concluded, is regarded as inevitable."—Daily Papers.

40 A cartoon in the 'Manchester Daily Despatch' of 19 March 1904, shortly before Churchill crossed to the Liberal benches. The chicken in the Liberal hen-coop is Sir Henry Campbell-Bannerman, then Leader of the Opposition.

THE NEW BOY.

OLIVER CHURCHILL BEGINS A NEW CAREER.

41 A cartoon in the 'Pall Mall Gazette' of 7 June 1904, after Churchill had joined the Liberals. Campbell-Bannerman is at the stove, with John Morley (standing) and H. H. Asquith (seated) on his left. Lloyd George is seated, far right.

43 On 10 December 1905 Churchill became Under-Secretary of State for the Colonies in Campbell-Bannerman's Liberal Government. On 13 January 1906 he was elected as Member of Parliament for Manchester North-West. During 1906 he played a leading part in the conciliation of South Africa. He is seen here at the meeting of Colonial Prime Ministers, held in London on 8 May 1907. Asquith is sitting below him, Lloyd George at the far right. On Churchill's left are the Permanent Under-Secretary of State at the Colonial Office, Sir Francis Hopwood, and the South African Prime Minister Louis Botha (to whose daughter, it was rumoured in the press – Churchill had become engaged). The Colonial Secretary, Lord Elgin, is seated at the centre of the group (with white beard).

42 Churchill entrusted his literary earnings to the banker, Sir Ernest Cassel, telling him: '*feed my sheep*'. Under Cassel's guidance, Churchill's investments prospered. This photograph shows Churchill and Cassel together in 1906. After his death in September 1921 Churchill wrote to Cassel's granddaughter Edwina (later Lady Mountbatten): '*He was a valued friend of my father's & I have taken up that friendship & have held it all my grown life. I had the knowledge that he was vy fond of me & believed in me at all times – especially in hard times. I had a real & deep affection for him. . . .*'

44 to 50 Churchill with his constituents, at a garden party in Manchester, 23 August 1907.

51 As Under-Secretary of State for the Colonies, Churchill decided to visit East Africa. He travelled out in October 1907, through Malta and Cyprus, combining work, sightseeing and hunting. Here he is in Malta, in formal dress with his Private Secretary, Eddie Marsh, who served with him in every Government office that he held from 1905 to 1929. Marsh often advised Churchill not to send letters and telegrams which he believed were best unsent. On 4 January 1906 Churchill's aunt Leonie Leslie had written to him: '*I heard of you through Mr Marsh and I am so glad you make "si bon menage" together. He seems delighted to be with you – and already fond of you! Which is a good thing, as one can work so much better for anyone one cares for.*' Twenty years later, on 2 May 1928, T. E. Lawrence wrote to a friend about Marsh: '*. . . many people despise him; I've found him sincere always; and he serves Winston with all his might.*'

52 Churchill and Marsh on horseback in the Sudan. On 6 November 1907, Churchill wrote to his mother: '*What a difference to the fag of a London day. My heart bounds up with every day I spend in the open air.*'

53
On arrival at Mombasa station, Churchill was greeted by the Colony's officials, and watched by the settlers. In his letter to his mother of 6 November, he wrote: '*Everything moves on the smoothest of wheels for me. A special train with dining & sleeping cars was at my disposal all the way. Whenever I wished to stop, it stopped.*'

Churchill sailed o
the Nile at Kha
toum, and visite
the battlefield o
Omdurman, whe
he had foug
twelve years befor
While at Khartou
his manservar
Scrivings, die
suddenly of foo
poisoning. After tl
funeral, Church
wrote to his mothe
'It was a melancho
& startling event;
to me who ha
become so depe
dent upon this po
man for all the lit
intimate comforts
my daily life, it h
been a most keen
palpable loss...
thought as I walk
after the coffin
Khartoum – I alwa
follow funera
there – how easily
might have bee
might then still l
m

54 At Khartoum, Churchill visited the buildings which had been shelled during the war of 1898, in which he had fought as a young officer. Here he poses in front of a shell-scarred wall. The city had been bombarded in 1898 by British gunboats which had sailed up the Nile. During his journey of 1907, Churchill sent several dozen long memoranda back to the Colonial Office. One senior civil servant there, Sir Francis Hopwood, wrote to the Colonial Secretary, Lord Elgin, about Churchill: '*He is most tiresome to deal with & will I fear give trouble – as his father did – in any position to which he may be called. The restless energy, uncontrollable desire for notoriety & the lack of moral perception make him an anxiety indeed!!*'

56 On 5 April 1908 H. H. Asquith became Prime Minister, and seven days later Churchill entered the Cabinet as President of the Board of Trade. Because of his appointment, he had to stand for re-election to Parliament. This photograph shows him campaigning in his constituency. Manchester North-West. But on 23 April he was defeated by his unsuccessful Conservative opponent of two years previously. To Miss Clementine Hozier, with whom he had fallen in love, he wrote on 27 April: '*I am glad to think you watched the battle from afar with eye sympathetic to my fortunes. Now I have to begin all over again. . . .*'

Daily Mirror

THE MORNING JOURNAL WITH THE SECOND LARGEST NET SALE.

No. 1,414. Registered at the G.P.O. as a Newspaper.   MONDAY, MAY 11, 1908.   One Halfpenny.

MR. WINSTON CHURCHILL FINDS "A SAFE SEAT" AT LAST: REJECTED IN MANCHESTER, HE IS ELECTED M.P. FOR DUNDEE.

57 Churchill soon found a new constituency, Dundee, for which he was elected on 9 May 1908. The 'Daily Mirror' of 11 May recorded his success.

59 Churchill became a Privy Councillor on 1 May 1907; here he is seen with John Morley in Privy Council uniform, on their way to St James's Palace, 6 July 1908.

58 Churchill in 1908.

60

In 1908, on his return from East Africa, Churchill joined the Cabinet, as President of the Board of Trade. Aged thirty-three, he was one of the youngest Cabinet Ministers of his time. Four months after entering the Cabinet, he became engaged to Miss Clementine Hozier. In a letter to his bride-to-be, on 8 August 1908, he described himself as *'stupid and clumsy'* in his relations with women, and *'quite self-reliant and self-contained'*.

61 A photograph of Miss Clementine Hozier, taken during her engagement. On 12 August 1908 Churchill wrote to his future mother-in-law, Lady Blanche Hozier: '*I am not rich nor powerfully established, but your daughter loves me & with that love I feel strong enough to assume this great & sacred responsibility; & I think I can make her happy & give her a station & career worthy of her beauty & virtues.*'

Zur Vermählung des englischen Handelsministers.

Mrs. Winston Churchill, geb. Miß Clementine Hozier. Oben: Mr. Winston Churchill.

62 A German newspaper illustration, after Churchill's wedding on 12 September 1908. On the following day Churchill wrote to his mother *'What a relief to have got that ceremony over! & so happily.'*

63

Churchill on his wedding day: arriving at St Margaret's, Westminster, with his best man, Lord Hugh Cecil. Lloyd George was among those who signed the register. The Churchills spent their honeymoon first at Blenheim, then at Baveno on Lake Maggiore, and finally in Venice.

64

Churchill and his wife during their first year of marriage. On 6 September 1909 he wrote to her: '*I am so much centred in my politics, that I often feel I must be a dull companion, to anyone who is not in the trade too. It gives me so much joy to make you happy – & I often wish I were more various in my topics.*'

65 Churchill and Lloyd George (top left) watch a demonstration of the Brennan Monorail at the White City on 4 November 1910. Augustine Birrell is standing below Lloyd George. Asquith, his daughter Violet, Sir Ernest Cassel, and Clementine Churchill were also present. This is one of the only photographs showing Churchill and Lloyd George together before 1911. At the end of 1908 Churchill had joined Lloyd George in opposing the increased naval expenditure demanded by the First Lord of the Admiralty, Reginald McKenna, for they were both strongly opposed to the creation of an arms race with Germany, and wanted to concentrate Government spending on social reform. In 1886 Lord Randolph had resigned over the Government's military expenditure, and had never held public office again. On 21 December 1908 Lloyd George wrote to Churchill: '*I cannot go away without expressing to you my deep obligation for the assistance you rendered me in smashing McKenna's fatuous estimates & my warm admiration for the splendid way in which you tore them up. I am a Celt & you will forgive me for telling you that the whole time you were raking McK's squadron I had a vivid idea in my mind that your father looked on with pride at the skilful & plucky way in which his brilliant son was achieving victory in a cause for which he had sacrificed his career & his life.*'

66
Churchill and
McKenna on
their way to a
Cabinet meeting
at the end of
1909.

67 Churchill was a keen supporter of the Territorial Army. Here four members of the Churchill family pose for a photograph at a Territorial camp of the Queen's Own Oxfordshire Hussars: The 9th Duke of Marlborough, Viscount Churchill, Winston Churchill and Jack Churchill. Churchill went every year to camp and to manœuvres. On 15 September 1909, while a guest at manœuvres in Germany, he wrote to his wife: '*Much as war attracts & fascinates my mind with its tremendous situations – I feel more deeply every year – & can measure the feeling here in the midst of arms – what vile & wicked folly & barbarism it all is.*'

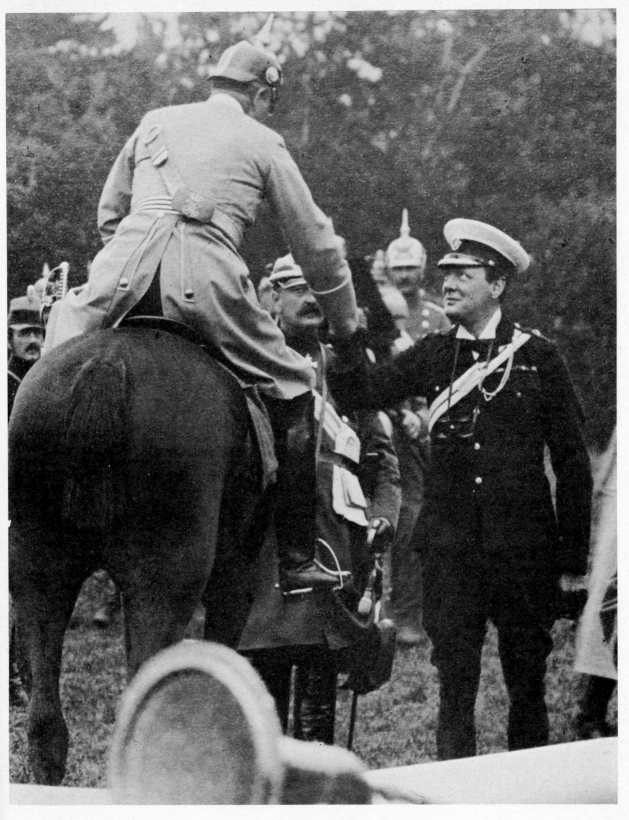

68 While at manœuvres in Germany, Churchill was the guest of the Kaiser, with whom he is here seen shaking hands.

A MINISTER "CAPTURED" BY A SUFFRAGETTE:
MR. WINSTON CHURCHILL AND MISS MAY DREW.

Miss Drew was one of the Suffragettes who visited the House of Commons
the other day, and was more fortunate than some of her sisters in the
cause, for she "captured" Mr. Winston Churchill as that Minister was
leaving the House, walked with him for a considerable distance, and
"lectured" him the while. Mr. Churchill "bore up" well under the strain,
and appeared interested.—[PHOTOGRAPH BY L.N.A.]

69 A page from the 'Illustrated London News', 10 April 1909.

70 On 14 November 1909 a militant suffragette, Miss Theresa Garnett, attacked Churchill with a dog whip at Bristol railway station. The blow caught him across the face, and also dented his hat. As detectives pulled her away, she called out: '*You brute, why don't you treat British women properly?*' Two days later the 'Manchester Evening News' published this drawing of the incident. On 12 July 1910 Churchill spoke, and voted, against the Bill to give women the vote. Suffragette threats continued. On 1 February 1913 Churchill wrote to his wife: '*Be vy careful not to open suspicious parcels arriving by post. . . . On the other hand do not leave them lying unopened in the house. They shd be dealt with carefully & promptly. These harpies are quite capable of trying to burn us out.*'

71 Throughout his two years at the Board of Trade, Churchill had been a strong advocate of
State aid to the sick and the unemployed. Among his measures was the setting up of Labour
Exchanges, to help the unemployed to find work. On 1 February 1910 he and his wife
visited the first seventeen Labour Exchanges, all of which had been opened that day. This
picture shows them at the Whitechapel Exchange. Nearly two years earlier, on 14 March
1908, he had written to Asquith: '*Dimly across gulfs of ignorance I see the outline of a policy
wh I call the Minimum Standard. . . . Underneath, though not in substitution for, the immense
disjoined fabric of social safeguards & insurances which has grown up by itself in England, there
must be spread – at a lower level – a sort of Germanised network of State intervention &
regulation.*'

72 Sir Edward Grey, Churchill and Lord Crewe coming away from a Cabinet meeting following the Liberal victory in the General Election of 14 February 1910. The election had been fought by the Liberals in order to challenge the House of Lords, which had been blocking much of the Liberals' social legislation. In the campaign, Churchill travelled throughout the country denouncing the powers of the Lords. On 1 February 1910, at the height of the campaign, Asquith had written to Churchill: '*Your speeches from first to last have reached a high-water mark, and will live in history.*' In one of these speeches, made at Leven on 9 January 1910, Churchill had declared, of Lord Lansdowne: '*His career represents privilege and favour from beginning to end; consistent and unbroken spoon-feeding from start to finish—that is the royal road to favour and employment. He is the representative of a played out, obsolete, anachronistic Assembly, a survival of a feudal arrangement utterly passed out of its original meaning – a force long since passed away, which only now requires a smashing blow from the electors to finish it for ever.*' On the day of the election victory, Churchill was appointed Home Secretary. He was thirty-five years old.

73 Mrs Lloyd George, Lloyd George, Churchill and William Clarke (Lloyd George's Secretary), on the way to the House of Commons for Lloyd George's Budget, 27 April 1910. Churchill wanted strong measures against the House of Lords if it rejected the Budget. '*The time has come for the total abolition of the House of Lords*', he had written to Asquith on 14 February 1910. The Budget passed the House of Commons by 324 votes to 231; the House of Lords, accepting the verdict of the election, agreed to it without even a division. That night Churchill wrote to Edward VII: '*Everyone is tired out by the unceasing strain, and the holiday of a month is the dearest wish of most Members of the House of Commons.*'

74

A cartoon by Max Beerbohm, 1910. Churchill, standing in the grounds of Blenheim Palace, is saying to his cousin, the Duke of Marlborough: '*Come come! As I said in one of my speeches, "there is nothing in the Budget to make it harder for a poor hard-working man to keep a decent home in comfort"*.'

75 Churchill and his cousin the Duke of Marlborough go to Buckingham Palace on 6 May 1910, the day after the death of Edward VII, to attend the Privy Council meeting on the accession of the new King, George V. On 10 February 1911 Churchill wrote to George V advocating Labour Colonies for '*tramps and wastrels*', and commenting: '*It must not however be forgotten that there are idlers and wastrels at both ends of the social scale.*' The King intimated in reply that he regarded the proposal as '*socialistic*' and the comment as '*superfluous*'.

20 TURN 'EM OUT!

20

(Copyright.)

76 A playing card designed by E. T. Reed, the 'Punch' cartoonist, for the game of 'PANKO or VOTES FOR WOMEN'. The game took the form of 'Suffragists v. Anti-Suffragists'. Churchill is shown in his Privy Councillor's robes.

77 Churchill's first child, Diana, was born on 11 July 1909. On 12 September he wrote to his wife: '*I wonder what she will grow into, & whether she will be lucky or unlucky to have been dragged out of chaos. She ought to have some rare qualities both of mind & body. But these do not always mean happiness or peace.*' Four months later there was a brief moment of friction between husband and wife, and on 10 November he wrote to her: '*Dearest it worries me vy much that you should seem to nurse such absolutely wild suspicions wh are so dishonouring to all the love & loyalty I bear you & will please god bear you while I breathe. They are unworthy of you & me. And they fill my mind with feelings of embarrassment to wh I have been a stranger since I was a schoolboy. . . . You ought to trust me for I do not love & will never love any woman in the world but you and my chief desire is to link myself to you week by week by bonds which shall ever become more intimate & profound. Beloved I kiss your memory – your sweetness & beauty have cast a glory upon my life.*'

78 Churchill's second child, Randolph – his only son – was born on 28 May 1911. Five days later Churchill wrote, to his wife, from Blenheim Park where he was in camp with the Oxfordshire Hussars: *'Many congratulations are offered me upon the son. With that lack of jealousy wh ennobles my nature, I lay them all at your feet.'* And he added that he hoped that his son would not be backward in his feeding. *'At his age'*, he explained, *'greediness & even swinishness at table are virtues.'* This photograph shows Churchill and his son together at the seaside in the summer of 1912.

81 Postcards of 'The Battle of Stepney' were sold in large numbers, and the incident was recorded in an early cinema newsreel. This photograph was circulated widely as a postcard. Eddie Marsh is standing next to Churchill (both in top hats). In the House of Commons the Conservative Leader, A. J. Balfour, criticized Churchill's action: '*He was, I understand in military phrase, in what is known as the zone of fire – he and a photographer were both risking valuable lives. I understand what the photographer was doing, but what was the right honourable gentleman doing?*'

79 Scots Guards covering 100 Sidney Street, a house in the East End of London where two armed burglars were trapped on 3 January 1911. The burglars had killed three of the policemen who tried to arrest them, and had begun to fire on the police from the house. Because the burglars had rifles and the police were only armed with revolvers, Churchill had – at the request of the War Office – given authority for a detachment of Scots Guards to go to the scene.

80 Churchill himself arrived in Sidney Street shortly after the soldiers. Later that day he wrote, to Asquith: '*It was a striking scene in a London street – firing from every window, bullets chipping the brickwork, police and Scots Guards armed with loaded weapons artillery brought up etc.*' In a note written seven days later he recalled: '*I made it my business, however, after seeing what was going on in front to go round the back of the premises and satisfy myself that there was no chance of the criminals effecting their escape through the intricate area of walls and small houses at the back of No 100 Sidney Street. This took some time, and when I returned to the corner of Sidney Street I was told that the house had caught on fire, and I could see smoke coming out from the top-floor window.*'

82 The fire at 100 Sidney Street. In his letter to Asquith, Churchill wrote: '*I thought it better to let the House burn down than spend good British lives in rescuing those ferocious rascals.*' After the fire had burnt itself out the police entered the building, and found two bodies. One had been shot, the other asphyxiated.

83

Churchill giving evidence at the Sidney Street inquest on 18 January 1911. He had been much criticized in the Press for having conducted the operation and given orders to the police and firemen. He told the Coroner: '*A junior officer of the Fire Brigade (Station Officer Edmonds) came up to me where I was standing and said that the Fire Brigade had arrived, and that he understood he was not to put out the fire at present. Was this right? or words to that effect. I said, "Quite right; I accept full responsibility." I wish to make it clear that these words refer to the specific question asked me, and that I confirmed and supported the police in their action. From what I saw, it would have meant loss of life and limb to any fire brigade officer who had gone within effective range of the building. . . . I did not in any way direct or over-ride the arrangements that the police authorities had made. I gave no directions to alter arrangements already made by them.*' Sydney Holland (later Viscount Knutsford), who was with Churchill throughout the siege, wrote to him six days before the Inquest: '*The only possible excuse for anyone saying that you gave orders is that you did once and very rightly go forward and wave back the crowd at the far end of the road. If those miscreants had come out there would have been lots of people shot by the soldiers. And you did also give orders that you and I were not to be shot in our hindquarters by a policeman who was standing with a 12 bore behind you!*'

84 Churchill talking to Lord Northcliffe at the Hendon Aviation Meeting, 12 May 1911. Clementine Churchill is on the left, shielding her eyes. Churchill was an early and eager advocate of flying. As early as 25 February 1909 he had told the Aerial Navigation sub-Committee of the Committee of Imperial Defence that the problem of the use of aeroplanes '*was a most important one*', and he had urged his colleagues to avail themselves of the Wright Brothers' expertise. At the Hendon Meeting Churchill watched the aviator Grahame-White drop a bomb on an area marked out to resemble the deck of a ship. The demonstration was organised by the Parliamentary Aerial Defence Committee.

85 Churchill and McKenna (in top hat) at the Hendon Aviation Meeting. The hatless man is the pilot and aeroplane instructor Grahame-White. On 24 October 1911 Churchill left the Home Office to become First Lord of the Admiralty. As First Lord he devoted much energy to building up the Royal Naval Air Service and was encouraged in his decision by Admiral of the Fleet Lord Fisher (then retired), who wrote to him on 10 November 1911: '*Aviation supersedes small cruisers & Intelligence vessels. You told me you would push aviation – you are right. . . .*' Churchill responded readily to Fisher's enthusiasm. Over two years earlier in a letter to his wife on 30 May 1909, he had described – after attending an Army Field Day in Berkshire – his attitude to military, naval and air matters: '*These military men vy often fail altogether to see the simple truths underlying the relationships of all armed forces, & how the levers of power can be used upon them. Do you know I would greatly like to have some practice in the handling of large forces. I have much confidence in my judgment on things, when I see clearly, but on nothing do I seem to feel the truth more than in tactical combinations. It is a vain and foolish thing to say – but you will not laugh at it. I am sure I have the root of the matter in me. . . .*'

87 Lord Fisher and Churchill on their way to the launching of HMS 'Centurion', 18 November 1911. This was the first King George V Class battleship to be launched after Churchill became First Lord. Six months later Churchill persuaded Fisher to become Chairman of the Royal Commission on Oil Supply, writing to him on 11 June 1912: '*This liquid fuel problem has got to be solved, and the natural inherent, unavoidable difficulties are such that they require the drive and enthusiasm of a big man. . . . You have got to find the oil: to show how it can be stored cheaply: how it can be purchased regularly and cheaply in peace; and with absolute certainty in war. . . . I recognize it is little enough I can offer you. But your gifts, your force, your hopes, belong to the Navy, with or without return; and as your most sincere admirer, and as the head of the Naval Service, I claim them now, knowing well you will not grudge them. You need a plough to draw. Your propellers are racing in air.*'

86 Churchill as First Lord of the Admiralty; a photograph taken at the time of his appointment on 24 October 1911, five weeks before his thirty-fifth birthday. Four days later the 'Observer' declared: '*We are afraid of Mr Churchill because he is weak and rhetorical . . . his moods are not to be depended upon. We cannot detect in his career any principles or even any consistent outlook upon public affairs. His ear is always to the ground; he is the true demagogue, sworn to give the people what they want, or rather, and that is infinitely worse, what he fancies they want. No doubt he will give the people an adequate Navy if they insist upon it.*' This was typical of Conservative comment at the time.

88 Churchill with Prince Louis of Battenberg (Second Sea Lord, 1911–12). This photograph shows them at Dover on 25 April 1912, when they inspected the harbour defences. On 29 October 1914, after Prince Louis had resigned as First Sea Lord, Churchill wrote to him: *'The Navy of today, and still more the Navy of tomorrow, bears the imprint of your work.'*

...hurchill on board the Royal yacht 'Victoria and ...lbert', at Spithead, 9 July 1912, for the Naval ...eview. Asquith was also present, and that evening ...hurchill wrote to his wife: '*The PM is quite in-* *fatigable & has been on his legs all day. He loves* ...*is sort of life & is well suited to it. He would have* ...*ade a much better Admiral than most I have to get* ...*ong with. Prince Louis looked vy imposing on his* ...*lendid Thunderer.*' Churchill spent several months ...sea each year, in 1912, 1913 and 1914, mostly on ...oard the Admiralty yacht 'Enchantress'. On ...January 1913 he wrote to his wife from the Firth ...Tay: '*I wish you were here. . . . Don't be disloyal* ...*me in thought. I have no one but you to break the* ...*neliness of a bustling and bustled existence.*' And ...2 November 1913 he wrote to her from Port-...nd: '*We are an enormous crowd on board and* *ery cabin chock full. . . . Wind & rain & sea =* *owds of men talking shop = cold & sleet = more* ...*op. But it amuses me – I am a fool who shd not have* ...*en born.*'

...O

...ady Randolph Churchill, her son, and Eddie ...Marsh at Earls Court on Armada Day, 29 July ...912, on board a model of Sir Francis Drake's ...ip 'Revenge'.

91 Holiday time. Churchill at Cannes, setting off for golf with the American actress Maxine Elliot, February 1913.

92 Golfing at Cannes.

93 Clementine Churchill, her husband, and Millicent Duchess of Sutherland on the front at Monte Carlo, February 1913.

94 Churchill and his wife arriving at the Channel Islands, 1913, having just landed from the 'Enchantress'.

THE "OFFICIAL" TOUR ENDED

Mr. Asquith and Mr. Winston Churchill arriving at Victoria Station
last week on their return from the Mediterranean

95 During May 1913 Churchill steamed on the 'Enchantress' to the Eastern Mediterranean and
the Adriatic, visiting British naval squadrons and stations. Among those who went with him
was the Prime Minister, H. H. Asquith. This photograph was published in the 'Bystander',
on 4 June 1913.

UNDER HIS MASTER'S EYE.

SCENE—*Mediterranean, on board the Admiralty yacht "Enchantress."*

MR. WINSTON CHURCHILL. "ANY HOME NEWS?"

MR. ASQUITH. "HOW CAN THERE BE WITH YOU HERE?"

96 A cartoonist's view of the cruise of the 'Enchantress'. This cartoon appeared in 'Punch' on 21 May 1913. (In December 1908 Churchill had published an account of his African tour, entitled 'My African Journey'; in this cartoon the book at his side is called 'My journey in Africa'.)

Churchill's two children, Randolph (in pram) and Diana, walking with their nannies out- **99**
side Admiralty House. In 1913 an unsuccessful attempt was made by suffragettes to kidnap
the young Randolph (then aged two) from his pram. Churchill was devoted to his two
children. On 23 July 1913 he wrote to his wife, from on board the 'Enchantress': *'Tender
love to you my sweet one & to both those little kittens & especially that radiant Randolph.
Diana is a darling too: & I repent to have expressed a preference. But somehow he seems a more
genial generous nature: while she is mysterious and self conscious. They are vy beautiful &
will win us honour some day when everyone is admiring her & grumbling about him.'*

7 General Sir Ian Hamilton, Churchill, his brother Jack, and his close friend, the Conservative MP F. E. Smith, at Buckingham in September 1913, during Army manœuvres.

8 Clementine Churchill, Admiral Hood (Churchill's Naval Secretary), Churchill and Eddie
Marsh at Lords. Admiral Hood was killed at the Battle of Jutland in 1916.

100

Churchill and Lord Fisher leaving a meeting of th
Committee of Imperial Defence in 1913. Fisher er
couraged Churchill to press his colleagues for sub
stantial increases in British naval power. On 2
August 1913 Churchill drew up detailed plans t
create a War Fleet of 79 battleships by 192
(instead of the 59 which up till then had bee
planned for). He believed that if such a fleet wer
built, the Germans would be deterred from takin
any aggressive action which might involve Britair
But at the same time Churchill offered to halt thi
programme if the Germans were willing, for thei
part, to accept a 'naval holiday'. The Germa
Government refused his offer.

101

Churchill with his friend Jack Seely (then Secretary
of State for War) watching the Review of the
Brigade of Guards in Hyde Park, 28 April 1913.

102 A German view of Churchill's naval policy, published in the weekly magazine 'Ulk' on
28 November 1913. Churchill's veils are marked '*For an increase in the navy*' and '*Against an
increase in the navy*', and the caption reads: '*What then will result from Churchill's dance of
the veils? A naked egoist!*'

The problem of the hour. What shall we give? Christmas presents for notabilities. — No. 1.

103 A cartoonist's view of Churchill's flying activities. This cartoon was published in the 'Birmingham Evening Despatch' on 1 December 1913. Throughout 1913 and 1914 Churchill learned to fly, and at the same time worked to improve the performance of aeroplanes, and the power of the Royal Naval Air Service. In a letter to his wife on 23 October 1913, after a day of flying practice, he wrote: '*It is vy satisfactory to find such signs of progress in every branch of the Naval air service. In another year – if I am spared ministerially – there will be a gt development. When I have pumped in another million the whole thing will be alive & on the wing.*'

104 and 105 Two photographs of Churchill on 23 February 1914, after he had gone on a practice flight at Eastchurch. The weekends which he spent flying were a delight to him. After an earlier practice on 23 October 1913 he wrote to his wife: '*It has been as good as one of those old days in the S. African war, & I have lived entirely in the moment, with no care for all those tiresome party politics & searching newspapers, & awkward by-elections. . . . For good luck before I started I put your locket on.*'

106

Churchill on his way to the Cabinet, 22 January 1914. His proposals for increased Naval expenditure to meet the rapidly increased German naval construction, had provoked strong opposition from Lloyd George, and divided the Cabinet. The crisis continued for more than a month. On 26 January Churchill wrote to Lloyd George: *'While I am responsible, what is necessary will have to be provided. The estimate of 1914–15 have been prepared with the strictest economy. For all expenditure incurred or proposed there is full warrant & good reason. There is no act of Admiralty administration for which I am responsible wh cannot be vindicated to the House of Commons. I cannot buy a year of office by a bargain under duress about estimates of 1915–16. No forecasts beyond the year have ever been made by my predecessors; & I have no power – even if I were willing – to bind the Board of Admiralty of 1915 to any exact decision. I recognise your friendship, but I ask no favours & I shall enter into no irregular obligations.'*

10⟨

A cartoon by E. T. Reed, published in the 'B⟨ stander' on 28 January 1914, at the height of t⟨ naval estimates crisis. From left to right: Lloy⟨ George, Haldane, Asquith, Grey and Churchi⟨ Within two weeks the majority of Churchill's pr⟨ posals for a larger Navy had been accepted by t⟨ Cabinet. On 2 February Churchill wrote to Asquit⟨ *'I do not love this naval expenditure & am grieved ⟨ be found in the position of taskmaster. But I am m⟨ self the slave of facts & forces wh are uncontrollab⟨ unless naval efficiency is frankly abandoned. T⟨ result of all this pressure & controversy leaves r⟨ anxious chiefly lest the necessary services have be⟨ cut too low.'* On 10 February, when the crisis w⟨ over, Churchill wrote to his mother: '*. . . it has be⟨ a long and wearing business wh has caused me ⟨ times vy gt perplexity*'.

"We All Go the Same Way Home!"

THE ONLY QUESTION STANDING OVER FOR DECISION BEING——WHICH WAY IS IT?

108 Churchill on board ship at Dover, 8 April 1914, on his way to Spain, where he was to play Polo as the guest of King Alfonso.

109 Churchill on his polo pony during his visit to Spain. He also worked during his holiday, writing to Prince Louis of Battenberg from Madrid on 14 April 1914: '*Freedom from politics and pouches has enabled me to deal comprehensibly with the various Staff questions now pending & I have spent several days on the task. Will you kindly read my memo. . . .*'

110 Churchill crossing Horse Guards Parade.

111 In the summer of 1914 Churchill took Field-Marshal Sir John French (Commander-in-Chief designate of the British Expeditionary Force) to inspect naval installations in Scotland.

112 Churchill's support for expansion of the Royal Naval Air Service was vigorous and widely approved. This cartoon by Bernard Partridge, entitled 'Neptune's Ally', was published in 'Punch' on 25 May 1914, shortly after Churchill's return from Spain, when it was reported in the Press that he was continuing with his flying practice.

113 On 29 May 1914 Churchill wrote to his wife from Portsmouth: '*My darling one, I have been at the Central Flying School for a couple of days – flying a little in good & careful hands & under perfect conditions. So I did not write you from there as I know you wd be vexed.*' In her reply, Clementine Churchill begged him to stop flying altogether. He accepted her plea, writing from the 'Enchantress' on 6 June: '*I will not fly any more. . . .*' and adding: '*This is a wrench, because I was on the verge of taking my pilot's certificate. It only needed a couple of calm mornings; & I am confident of my ability to achieve it vy respectably. I shd greatly have liked to reach this point wh wd have made a suitable moment for breaking off. But I must admit that the numerous fatalities of this year wd justify you in complaining if I continued to share the risks – as I am proud to do – of these good fellows. So I give it up decidedly for many months & perhaps for ever. This is a gift – so stupidly am I made – wh costs me more than anything wh cd be bought with money. So I am vy glad to lay it at your feet, because I know it will rejoice & relieve your heart. Anyhow I can feel I know a good deal about this fascinating new art. I can manage a machine with ease in the air, even with high winds, & only a little more practice in landings wd have enabled me to go up with reasonable safety alone. I have been up nearly 140 times, with many pilots, & all kinds of machines, so I know the difficulties the dangers & the joys of the air – well enough to appreciate them, & to understand all the questions of policy wh will arise in the near future. . . . Though I had no need & perhaps no right to do it – it was an important part of my life during the last 7 months, & I am sure my nerve, my spirits & my virtue were all improved by it. But at your expense my poor pussy cat! I am so sorry.*'

114

Sir Edward Grey and Churchill walking across the Horse Guards Parade on the eve of war in 1914. Churchill insisted, against much Ministerial opposition, that it was in Britain's interest to support France to repel a German attack, and on 28 July he ordered the Fleet to take up its War Stations in the North Sea. That night he wrote to his wife: '*Everything tends towards catastrophe & collapse. I am interested, geared up & happy. Is it not horrible to be built like that? The preparations have a hideous fascination for me. I pray to God to forgive me for such fearful moods of levity.*'

115

'Full Steam Ahead'; a cartoon of Churchill by Poy, published on 4 August 1914. On 24 August, as the Germans swept through Belgium, Churchill telegraphed to Admiral Jellicoe: '*We have not entered this business without resolve to see it through. You may rest assured that our action will be proportionate to the gravity of the need. I have absolute confidence in the final result.*'

FULL STEAM AHEAD!

116 Churchill on the eve of war; a photograph published in the 'Tatler' on 12 August 1914, with
an inset photograph of Clementine Churchill.

WINSTON CHURCHILL,
NATUS 1874.

For Character Sketch, see page 551.

117 A drawing of Churchill, published in 'Everyman' on 21 August 1914, at a time when his decision to send the Fleet to its War Stations before the outbreak of war was widely praised. In the 'Everyman' 'Character Sketch', an anonymous Member of Parliament wrote of Churchill: '*Those who have worked with him declare that there never was a Minister of the Crown so eager and swift in his work; and if they find a fault in him as a worker it is that he is apt to forget that all men are not endowed with his high talents and amazing energy. In times of relaxation he is never idle, and in times of great pressure he spares neither himself nor those around him, but he has the supreme gift of making his assistants in all ranks give the best of their labour freely to the task of the moment. Rumour tells us that he is heartless in his ambition and careless of every interest but his own. To that description his own closest associates, political, official, and personal, give the lie; and they will tell you that he is at once the most exacting and the most generous chief whom they have ever served.*'

WINSTON IN THE WAR
He is only Forty!

By **T. P.**

COLONEL SEELY AND MR. CHURCHILL DRIVING THROUGH THE STREETS OF BESIEGED ANTWERP.

118 On 3 October the Belgians planned to evacuate Antwerp. With the approval of Lord Kitchener and Sir Edward Grey, Churchill hurried to the city to rally its Belgian and British defenders. This photograph was published on 12 December 1914 in 'Great Deeds of the War'. The article was by T. P. O'Connor, the Irish Nationalist MP. With Churchill is his friend General Seely, a former Liberal Secretary of State for War.

119

Churchill at Antwerp. For three days he took virtual charge of the defence, helping to delay the German advance. Both while he was at Antwerp, and on his return, Churchill asked Asquith to be relieved of his Office and given a military command. Asquith refused, writing to a friend (Venetia Stanley) on 7 October: '*He is a wonderful creature, with a curious dash of schoolboy simplicity . . . and what someone said of genius – "a zigzag streak of lightning in the brain".*'

120 Churchill's third child, Sarah, was born on the day he returned from Antwerp. This family photograph, taken at Admiralty House towards the end of 1914, shows Churchill, his daughter Diana, his wife, his daughter Sarah (on her mother's lap), his son Randolph, his mother, his nephew Peregrine, his sister-in-law Lady Gwendeline, his nephew John-George, and his brother Jack, home briefly on leave. In October 1914 Jack had gone to the front with the Queen's Own Oxfordshire Hussars. On 9 November Churchill wrote to him from the Admiralty: '*I feel so acutely the ignoble position of one who merely cheers from the bank the gallant efforts of the rowers. But I cannot stir. The combinations at this moment are of the highest interest and importance. . . . Have no fear for the result. We have got the dirty dogs tight. The end is a long way off: but it is certain, tho' not in sight. . . . My dear I am always anxious about you. It wd take the edge off much if I cd be with you. I expect I shd be vy frightened but I wd dissemble.*'

121 Churchill, Kitchener and Lloyd George: a cartoon by Poy, published on Churchill's 40th birthday, 30 November 1914. That day, Margot Asquith wrote in her diary: '*Winston Churchill was 40 today. . . . He has done a good deal for a man of forty. . . . He never shirks, hedges, or protects himself – though he thinks of himself perpetually. He takes huge risks. He is at his very best just now; when others are shrivelled with grief – apprehensive, silent, irascible and self-conscious morally; Winston is intrepid, valourous, passionately keen and sympathetic, longing to be in the trenches – dreaming of war, big, buoyant, happy, even. It is very extra-ordinary, he is a born soldier.*' On 5 December 1914 Asquith wrote to Venetia Stanley about a new plan with which Churchill was involved: '*His volatile mind is at present set on Turkey & Bulgaria, & he wants to organize a heroic adventure against Gallipoli and the Dardanelles. . . .*' In May 1915 when Churchill had been forced to leave the Admiralty, Lord Kitchener told him: '*Well there is one thing at any rate they cannot take from you. The Fleet was ready.*'

123 On 19 February 1915 the War Cabinet agreed that troops should be sent to the Dardanelles (though not in the quantities which Churchill believed were essential if success were to be assured). On 25 February George V and Churchill went to Blandford, in Dorset, where the King inspected the Royal Naval Division before it sailed to the Dardanelles. This photograph was made into a postcard for the troops to send home with a farewell message. On the following day Churchill warned the War Council that if further troops were not sent, Britain would find herself *'face to face with a disaster'*.

22

urchill in February 1915, at the time when he and his naval advisers were preparing their bitious plan of attack at the Dardanelles, in the hope of capturing Constantinople, cing Turkey to surrender and persuading the neutral Balkan States (Bulgaria, Greece d Rumania) to attack Germany and Austria–Hungary. The War Cabinet had approved plan (to attack with ships alone) on 13 January 1915, despite Churchill's vehement tests that troops would be needed to follow up any naval success.

IRATE PATIENT: "This is ruining my system. Turn off the tap or I'll murder somebody."
SUAVE ATTENDANT: "Ah, he feels it! Now for a little more pressure."

124 While the final plans were being made for the Dardanelles operation, the public applauded the Navy's success in setting up a blockade of the German ports, and driving all German ships from the Atlantic, the Pacific and the Indian Ocean. This cartoon, showing the Kaiser's discomfiture, was published in the 'Manchester Dispatch' on 19 February 1915.

A PET AVERSION.

[After the picture by Phiz, in "The Old Curiosity Shop," of Quilp and Kit's effigy.

125 A cartoon published in the 'Westminster Gazette' on 25 February 1915, showing the Kaiser in action against Churchill, with the Crown Prince watching. The caption read: '*Mr Winston Churchill has a prominent place in the hate of British Ministers expressed in Germany.*'

126 Churchill's brother Jack sailed for the Dardanelles on 13 March 1915, on the Staff of the military Commander-in-Chief, Sir Ian Hamilton. This photograph was taken some weeks after the troops had landed on the Gallipoli Peninsula on 25 April 1915.

127 At the Dardanelles, the naval attack of 18 March 1915 failed to break through the Turkish minefields, and the subsequent military landings of 25 April failed to gain more than a foothold on the rugged Gallipoli Peninsula. On 15 May Lord Fisher resigned and the Conservatives threatened to start the first controversial debate of the war. In the Cabinet crisis that followed, Asquith agreed to form a Coalition with the Conservatives, who, as a condition of their acceptance, demanded Churchill's removal from the Admiralty. Here he is seen, during the crisis, walking to 10 Downing Street. On the morning of 21 May Churchill wrote to Asquith: '*I did not believe it was possible to endure such anxiety. None of the ordinary strains of war – wh I have borne all these months – are comparable to this feeling. . . . I can only look to you. Let me stand or fall by the Dardanelles – but do not take it from my hands.*' Later than same day, Churchill accepted that his career as First Lord was over, writing to Asquith: '*I am grateful to you for yr kindness to me & belief in my vision of things.*'

Churchill walking across Horse Guards Parade with his successor as First Lord, the former Conservative Prime Minister, A. J. Balfour. On 26 May Churchill wrote to Balfour about the future of the Gallipoli campaign: '*The military operations shd proceed with all possible speed so that the period of danger may be shortened. Whatever force is necessary, can be spared, and can be used, shd be sent at once, & all at once. . . . Punishment must be doggedly borne.*'

"WHERE IS LANCASTER
AND WHAT IS A DUCHY?"

130 While at the Admiralty, Churchill had taken the initiative in pressing for an armoured, mechanical vehicle which could crush barbed wire and penetrate the German trench lines. On 28 June 1915 he and Lloyd George went to Wormwood Scrubs to watch the trial of the Killen–Strait barbed wire cutter, a forerunner of the tank. Churchill is half hidden behind the post; Lloyd George is in bowler hat. But Churchill felt acutely his lack of authority. On 20 September he wrote to his friend Jack Seely: '*It is odious to me to remain here watching sloth & folly, with full knowledge & no occupation.*'

129

On 27 May 1915 Churchill became Chancellor of the Duchy of Lancaster in Asquith's Coalition Government. It was a post without any real power. This photograph was printed in the 'Bystander' on 2 June. Clementine Churchill later recalled: '*When he left the Admiralty he thought he was finished. . . . I thought he would die of grief.*'

132 Churchill and his wife listen to Lord Kitchener at the Guildhall, 9 July 1915. Horatio Bottomley (hands clasped) is just behind Churchill. Kitchener appealed for further volunteers to serve on the western front. In Cabinet, Churchill argued – with Lloyd George's support – that it was essential to introduce conscription, but Kitchener insisted that the voluntary system was adequate. On 4 October 1915 Churchill threatened to resign from the Cabinet unless Kitchener were removed, writing to Asquith: '*The experiment of putting a great soldier at the head of the War Office in time of war has not been advantageous.*' Churchill argued that Lloyd George should be made Secretary of State for War, on account of his '*drive and penetrating insight*'. Asquith declined to make any such change.

131

Churchill with two of the Conservative Ministers who joined the Coalition in May 1915; Lord Lansdowne and Lord Curzon. He continued to advocate further military effort at the Dardanelles, writing to all his Cabinet colleagues on 18 June: '*There can be no doubt that we now possess the means and the power to take Constantinople before the end of the summer if we act with decision and with a due sense of proportion. The striking down of one of the three hostile Empires against which we are contending, and the fall to our arms of one of the most famous capitals in the world, with the results which must flow therefrom, will, conjoined with our other advantages, confer upon us a far-reaching influence among the Allies, and enable us to ensure their indispensable co-operation. Most of all, it will react on Russia. It will give the encouragement so sorely needed. It will give the reward so long desired. It will render a service to an Ally unparalleled in the history of nations. It will multiply the resources and open the channel for the re-equipment of the Russian armies. It will dominate the Balkan situation and cover Italy. It will resound through Asia. Here is the prize, and the only prize, which lies within reach this year. It can certainly be won without unreasonable expense, and within a comparatively short time. But we must act now, and on a scale which makes speedy success certain.*' But the renewed assault at Gallipoli, on 6 August, failed to drive the Turks from the Peninsula, and at the end of the year the British abandoned their attempts to break through to Constantinople.

133 to 136 Churchill and his wife at Enfield, 18 September 1915, when Churchill addressed munitions workers. During his speech he told them: '*We cannot understand the inscrutable purposes which have plunged these evils upon the world, and have involved all the nations of Europe in a catastrophe measureless in its horror. But we know that if in this time of crisis and strain we do our duty, we shall have done all that is in human power to do – and we shall so bear ourselves in this period – all us of, whatever part we play on the stage of the world's history – we shall bear ourselves so that those who come after us will find amid the signs and scars of this great struggle that the liberties of Europe and of Britain are still intact and inviolate; when those looking back upon our efforts such as they have been, will say of this unhappy but not inglorious generation, placed in a position of extraordinary trial, that it did not fail in the test, and that the torch which it preserved lights the world for us today.*'

137 Lloyd George and Churchill in Whitehall, October 1915. A month later Churchill was excluded from the newly formed inner War Cabinet, and resigned from the Government altogether, writing to Asquith on 11 November: '*I have a clear conscience which enables me to bear any responsibility for past events with composure. Time will vindicate my administration of the Admiralty, and assign me my due share in the vast series of preparations and operations which have secured us the command of the seas.*'

138 Having resigned from Asquith's Government, Churchill rejoined the Army and crossed to France, where he was attached for training to the Grenadier Guards. On 5 December 1915 he visited the French front line, together with his friend Captain Edward Louis Spears (third from left). On Churchill's left is General Fayolle (commanding the 33rd Corps), and behind the General is a German prisoner (in cap). That night Churchill wrote to his wife: '*I lunched with the HQ of the 33rd Corps and cheered them all up about the war & the future. The general insisted on our being photographed together – me in my French steel helmet – & to make a background German prisoners were lined up. . . .*' Churchill was full of admiration for Spears' bravery, writing to him a year later, in October 1916: '*I read your name this morning in the casualty list for the 4th time with keen emotion. . . . I cannot tell you how much I admire and reverence the brilliant & noble service you are doing & have done for the country. You are indeed a Paladin worthy to rank with the truest knights of the great days of romance. Thank God you are alive. Some good angel has guarded you amid such innumerable perils & brought you safely thus far along this terrible & never ending road.*'

139 On 4 January 1916 Churchill was appointed Lieutenant-Colonel, commanding the 6th Royal Scots Fusiliers. For six months he commanded them, first in training, then in the front line. This photograph, taken in Armentieres on 11 February, shows him with his 2nd in command, Sir Archibald Sinclair. Four days later Churchill wrote to his wife: '*Last night . . . after dinner, I had a splendid walk with Archie all over the top of the ground. We left the trenches altogether & made a thorough examination of all the fields, tracks, ruins etc immediately behind our line. You cannot show yourself here by day, but in the bright moonlight it is possible to move about without danger (except from random bullets) & to gain a vy clear impression. Archie was a vy good guide. We also went out in front of our own parapet into the No man's land & prowled about looking at our wire & visiting our listening posts. This is always exciting.*'

141

Humiliated by the hostile re-action to his speech, Churchill returned to the front. This photograph shows him in London on the eve of his return. Depressed at the turn of events, he wrote to his wife on 26 March 1916, from the trenches: '*So much effort, so many years of ceaseless fighting & worry, so much excitement & now this rough fierce life here under the hammer of Thor, makes my older mind turn for – the first time I think to other things than action. . . . Sometimes also I think I wd not mind stopping living vy much. I am so devoured by egoism that I wd like to have another soul in another world & meet you in another setting. . . . But I am not going to give in or tire at all. I am going on fighting to the vy end in any situation open to me from wh I can most effectively drive on this war to victory.*'

140

Churchill as Lieutenant-Colonel, 6th Royal Scots Fusiliers. On 6 March 1916, while he was in London on leave, he went to the House of Commons and denounced the Government's conduct of the naval war, warning MPs that: '*Blood and money, however lavishly poured out, would never repair the consequences of what might be even an unconscious relaxation of effort. . . . To lose momentum is not merely to stop but to fall.*' On 8 March Margot Asquith wrote to A. J. Balfour: '*I've never varied in my opinion of Winston I'm glad to say. He is a hound of the lowest sense of political honour, a fool of the lowest judgement & contemptible. He cured me of oratory in the House & bored me with oratory in the home.*'

The Right Hon. Winston S. Churchill, M.P.

143 Churchill speaking at Chelmsford, 9 September 1916. For six months he had argued in favour of a more vigorous conduct of the war, and had also sought to defend himself from the hostile cry: '*What about the Dardanelles?*', which was hurled at him on many public occasions. During his speech at Chelmsford he said: '. . . *in all classes of our countrymen there is no division of opinion as to what the ultimate outcome will be.* [Hear, hear.] *The great strength which our country has shown is a source of pride to everyone. The unanimity with which our Empire has rallied to the Mother Land in the great cause justifies and vindicates British institutions.* [Applause.] *It is over two years since the war began, and I well remember feeling at that time profoundly convinced that in declaring war on Germany our country had performed the most noble deed in all its history.* [Applause.] *We have gone through a lot since then: terrible losses, many disasters, bitter disappointments, but I never felt more sure than now, on this fine autumn afternoon, that the course we took two years ago was absolutely right –* [cheers] *– and that our children will live to bless the day and to glorify the deed.* [Loud cheers.]' On 7 December, Lloyd George replaced Asquith as Prime Minister. Churchill did not receive a place in the new Government; several Conservatives, including Lord Curzon, had insisted upon his exclusion.

142

Churchill returned to London from the western front in May 1916. Asquith did not offer him a place in the Government. On 15 July he wrote to his brother: '*Is it not damnable that I should be denied all real scope to serve this country, in this tremendous hour? Though my life is full of comfort, pleasure & prosperity, I writhe hourly not to be able to get my teeth effectively into the Boche. . . . Jack my dear I am learning to hate.*'

**144
and
145** In July 1917, despite strong Conservative opposition, Lloyd George appointed Churchill Minister of Munitions. For over a year he supervised the production of guns, tanks, aeroplanes and munitions. These photographs show him at Beardmore's Gun Works in Glasgow on 8 October 1918. Any defeatism, he told a public meeting in Glasgow that day, *'should be stamped out . . . with all the vigour of public opinion'.*

146 Churchill in Lille, 29 October 1918, watching a march past of British troops who had liberated the town eleven days before. Eddie Marsh is standing behind him (in bowler hat). Two days later, on 30 October, Turkey surrendered, followed by Austria–Hungary on 3 November and Germany on 11 November – '*a drizzle of empires*', Churchill told Marsh, '*falling through the air*'.

147 On 10 January 1919 Churchill became Secretary of State for War. A month later, on 14 February he went to the Paris Peace Conference with Field Marshal Sir Henry Wilson (Chief of the Imperial General Staff) to urge upon the French and Americans the need for a military expedition against the Russian Bolsheviks. But they were insistent that no Allied invasion would take place. Churchill accepted their decision. On 19 February, after his return to London, he told an audience at the Mansion House: *'If Russia is to be saved, as I pray she may be saved, she must be saved by Russians. It must be by Russian manhood and Russian courage and Russian virtue that the rescue and regeneration of this once mighty nation and famous branch of the European family can alone be achieved. The aid which we can give to these Russian Armies – who we do not forget were called into the field originally during the German war to some extent by our inspiration and who are now engaged in fighting against the foul baboonery of Bolshevism – can be given by arms, munitions, equipment, and technical services raised upon a voluntary basis.'*

WINSTON'S BAG

HE HUNTS LIONS AND BRINGS HOME DECAYED CATS

148 Throughout 1919 Churchill tried to increase British arms supplies to the anti-Bolsheviks, and denounced Bolshevism in Parliament and in the Press. By the end of 1919 the War Office had sent over £100 million pounds of military supplies from Britain to Russia. But the anti-Bolshevik forces, despite British support, were unable to capture Petrograd or Moscow, and were finally defeated. Churchill's vociferous denunciation of the Bolsheviks provoked bitter comment; this cartoon, by the cartoonist Low, was published in the 'Star' on 21 January 1920.

149 In August 1919 Churchill went to Cologne, where he inspected the British Army of Occupation. Field-Marshal Sir Henry Wilson (Chief of the Imperial General Staff) is standing on Churchill's left, with Sir Archibald Sinclair (who had become Churchill's Military Secretary), between them.

**150
and
151** Inspecting British forces, Cologne, August 1919.

152 Churchill and the Prince of Wales (later King Edward VIII) at a luncheon party in the House of Commons, 5 June 1919, to honour the three American airmen who had flown the Atlantic from the United States to Portugal. Six years earlier, after Churchill had met the Prince of Wales at Balmoral, he wrote to his wife (on 20 September 1913): '*He is so nice, & we have made rather friends. They are worried a little about him, as he has become very spartan – rising at 6 & eating hardly anything. He requires to fall in love with a pretty cat. . . .*'

153

Churchill and his wife arrive at Lincolns Inn on 7 October 1919, when he was summoned to give evidence to the Royal Commission on Awards to Inventors, which was enquiring into the origins of the tank.

154

Churchill reading his evidence about the origins of the tank. In its report the Royal Commission declared (on 17 November 1919): '*In the first place the Commission desire to record their view that it was primarily due to the receptivity, courage and driving force of the Rt. Hon Winston Spencer Churchill that the general idea of the use of such an instrument of warfare as the Tank was converted into a practical shape.*' The report continued: '*Mr Winston Churchill has very properly taken the view that all his thought and time belonged to the State and that he was not entitled to make any claim for an award, even had he wished to do so.*'

155 In 1919 and 1920 Churchill was Secretary of State for Air, as well as for War. Here, at the Hendon Air Display on 8 July 1920, he stands with Lady Sykes (Bonar Law's daughter), her husband Sir Frederick Sykes (Controller-General of Civil Aviation) and the Chief of the Air Staff, Sir Hugh Trenchard. Both as Secretary for Air, and as Colonial Secretary (1921–22) Churchill was a strong advocate of an independent Air Force; and supported plans for many pioneer air policies, including the Cairo to Karachi air service, the Air Force Administration of Iraq, the development of long-range flying, and the use of aerial bombing as an instrument of imperial policy.

156

Relaxation: Churchill playing Polo at Roehampton, June 1920. Because he had badly dislocated his shoulder in India in 1894, he had to play polo with a strap round his right arm; but he continued to play until he was fifty-one years old. His last game was in Malta in 1926.

157 On 15 February 1921 Churchill became Colonial Secretary. Three weeks later he set off for Cairo, where, in conference with his Middle East advisers, he set up two Arab kingdoms (in Transjordan and Iraq) and confirmed Britain's promise to the Jews of a 'National Home' in Palestine. On Sunday 20 March Churchill, his wife, T. E. Lawrence (his adviser on Arab affairs) and Gertrude Bell visited the Pyramids, and were photographed on camels. Churchill also set up his easel and spent part of the day painting the Pyramids.

158 From Cairo, Churchill went to Jerusalem, where, on 28 March 1921, he informed the Emir Abdullah (who was to become King of Transjordan) that Palestine was to remain a British Mandate open to Jewish settlement. Here Churchill is seen, with Lawrence and Abdullah, during a break in their talks. Churchill then visited the Jewish settlement at Rishon-le-Zion. On 14 June, after his return to England, he told the House of Commons: '*I was driven into a fertile and thriving country estate, where the scanty soil gave place to good crops and good cultivation, and then to vineyards and finally to the most beautiful, luxurious orange groves, all created in 20 or 30 years by the exertions of the Jewish community who live there. . . . I defy anybody, after seeing work of this kind, achieved by so much labour, effort and skill, to say that the British Government, having taken up the position it has, could cast it all aside and leave it to be rudely and brutally overturned by the incursion of a fanatical attack by the Arab population from outside.*'

160

In October 1922 Churchill was defeated in the General Election, and for the first time in twenty-two years was no longer a Member of Parliament. With the defeat of Lloyd George's Coalition, he was also excluded from the Cabinet. He began to write his war memoirs, entitled 'The World Crisis', for which he received over £40,000 as an advance. At the same time he bought Chartwell, an Elizabethan manor house near Westerham, in Kent, for less than £5,000. Chartwell remained his home until his death. Churchill greatly extended the house, and even built an island. Here he is seen at his fishpond.

159

Churchill leaving one of the Irish Treaty Conferences at 10 Downing Street on 26 May 1922. For nearly a year he took a major part, first in the Treaty negotiations, then in seeking to reconcile the Irish leaders from both north and south, and finally in persuading the House of Commons to accept the establishment of the Irish Free State in Southern Ireland. On 16 February 1922 he told the House of Commons: '*For generations we have been wandering and floundering in the Irish bog; but at last we think that in this Treaty we have set our feet upon a pathway, which has already become a causeway – narrow, but firm and far-reaching. Let us march along this causeway with determination and circumspection, without losing heart and without losing faith. If Britain continues to march forward along that path, the day may come – it may be distant, but it may not be so distant as we expect – when, turning round, Britain will find at her side Ireland united, a nation, and a friend.*'

161 Throughout 1923 and 1924 Churchill tried to return to Parliament. He was defeated at West Leicester, at the General Election in December 1923, and stood next for the Abbey Division of Westminster. This photograph shows him at his London home in Sussex Square, at work with his secretary, Miss Fisher, on 6 March 1924, during the Abbey election campaign.

162 Churchill and his wife receive a copy of Churchill's election address during the Abbey campaign. Churchill's main platform was an attack on Socialism. He described himself officially as an 'Independent anti-Socialist' candidate, and told the Press on 7 March that he represented '*all who believed in enterprise, self-reliance, and civil liberty, as opposed to the tyrannous barbarism of the Marxian system*'.

OUR OWN MUSSOLINI

163 This cartoon was published in the 'Weekly Westminster' on 15 March, during the Abbey campaign. Its caption was written by the historian Philip Guedalla: '*High up on the short waiting-list of England's Mussolinis stands the name of Winston Spencer Churchill. . . . In a wild vision of the distant future we seem to see him marching black-shirted upon Buckingham Palace with a victorious army of genteel but bellicose persons who have at last set their elegantly shod feet upon the coarse neck of Labour.*' The picture on the wall alludes to the British battleships sunk at the Dardanelles.

164 The Abbey by-election. Churchill's car overtakes Labour supporters on polling day, 20 March 1924. In a poll of over 22,000, he was defeated by only 43 votes by the official Conservative candidate.

165 Churchill doffs his hat after his defeat at the Abbey by-election. His wife turns to look at the camera.

THE FIGHT FOR THE FAVOURITE.

Mr. Lloyd George. "HERE, I SAY, THIS IS MY MOUNT."
Mr. Winston Churchill. "NO, IT ISN'T. I THOUGHT OF IT FIRST."

166 Speaking at Liverpool on 8 May 1924, Churchill described Socialism as *'one of the most profound and mischievous delusions which can ever enter the brain of man'*. This cartoon appeared in 'Punch' on 4 June.

The Recruiting Parade.

167 This cartoon by Low was published in the 'Star' on 7 October 1924. Lord Rothermere and Lord Beaverbrook (far right) are holding up the anti-Sosh banner. Two weeks earlier, on 23 September 1924 Churchill had been adopted as a 'Constitutional and Anti-Socialist' candidate by the Epping Conservatives, and on 26 September he had appealed to an audience of Scottish Conservatives for Conservative and Liberal unity in the face of Socialism. The policy of Ramsay MacDonald's Labour Government, Churchill declared, was: *'Our bread for the Bolshevik serpent; our aid for foreigners of every country; our favours for Socialists all over the world who have no country; but for our own daughter States across the oceans, on whom the future of the British island and nation depends, only the cold stones of indifference, aversion and neglect. That is the policy with which the Socialist Government confronts us, and against that policy we will strive to marshall the unconquerable might of Britain.'*

168 and 169 Churchill and his wife during the Epping election campaign. In his election address, issued on 12 October 1924, he declared: *'Spellbound by the lure of Moscow, wire-pulled through subterranean channels, Mr Ramsay MacDonald and his associates have attempted to make the British nation accomplices in Bolshevist crimes.'* On 29 October he was elected by a majority of near 10,000, in a total poll of 33,000. In 1925 he rejoined the Conservative Party, which he had left twenty-one years earlier.

170 On 4 November 1924 the Conservative leader Stanley Baldwin replaced Ramsay Mac-Donald as Prime Minister; two days later he appointed Churchill as Chancellor of the Exchequer (although Churchill was still not a member of the Conservative Party). This photograph shows Churchill being driven to Buckingham Palace on 7 November to receive his seal of office from the King.

171 Churchill at Victoria Station, 7 January 1925, on his way to attend the Allied Financial Conference in Paris, With him is his political secretary, Lord Wodehouse (later Earl of Kimberley). Churchill tried to persuade the French to agree to a reduction in German reparations, and to persuade the Americans to reduce France's war debts. On 8 January he told the negotiators: '*Hope flies on wings, and Inter-Allied Conferences plod along dusty roads, but still the conviction exists that progress is being made towards the recognition of the unity and prosperity of Europe. . . .*'

172

Churchill leaving 11 Downing Street on 28 April 1925, on his way to the House of Commons to deliver his first budget speech, and to announce that Britain would return to the Gold Standard. In his budget, Churchill reduced income tax, increased death duties, and introduced pensions for widows and orphans. Stanley Baldwin told the Commons that Churchill's budget would bring *'hope and comfort to the aged, to the homes that are oppressed by sorrow'*. But the economist J. M. Keynes believed that the folly of a return to the Gold Standard would eventually obliterate all the benefits of the social legislation.

173 Churchill parking in Birdcage Walk, Westminster, 1925. As Chancellor of the Exchequer, he continually argued in favour of strict economy, warning the House of Commons on 7 August 1925: '*The day may come when the nation's whole scale of living must be reduced. If that day comes, Parliament must lay the burden equally on all classes.*' And he added: '*I am not invested with dictatorial powers. If I were I should be quite ready to dictate.*'

174

Churchill at 10 Downing Street on 3 May 1926, at the start of the General Strike. During the Strike he organized the printing of a Government newspaper, the 'British Gazette', and was a leading advocate of 'no surrender' to the strikers. On 19 May, when the Strike was over, the 'Daily Mail', after praising the courage of Stanley Baldwin and Lord Birkenhead declared: '*Nor can the services of Mr Winston Churchill be overlooked. His energy and initiative have never been more clearly shown in a great cause. His presence in the Cabinet at this juncture has been an undoubted source of strength.*' As soon as the strike was over, Churchill made great efforts to persuade the coal-owners to make concessions to the coal-miners but his efforts were in vain.

175 Churchill and his son Randolph during their visit to Italy in January 1927. During his visit, Churchill told the Italian Press: '*If I had been an Italian, I am sure I should have been wholeheartedly with you in your triumphant struggle against the bestial appetites and passions of Leninism.*' Of Mussolini he said: '*I could not help being charmed, like so many other people have been, by his gentle and simple bearing and by his calm, detached poise in spite of so many burdens and dangers.*'

176 Their Italian visit over, Churchill and his son were the guests of the Duke of Westminster at Foucarmont, in the Forest of Eu. This photograph shows them about to set off for a wild boar hunt on 31 January 1927.

177 On holiday at Deauville, 1 August 1927.

178
Randolph
Churchill
skating with his
mother on the
lake at
Chartwell during
the 'Great Snow'
of 1927–28.

179
Chartwell under
snow.
Churchill's study
is the room
with the bow
window, on the
extreme left.

Chu
puttin
finishing to
to his snow

181 Madame Chanel, Randolph Churchill (aged sixteen) and his father at the Duke of Westminster's boarhounds, Dampierre, France. During the inter-war years Churchill went almost every year to France, where several of his friends had houses and estates. There he hunted, painted, and wrote books. In England, he spent as much time as he could at Chartwell. From Chartwell, he wrote to his wife on 5 April 1928: *'I am becoming a Film fan, and last week I went to see "The Last Command", a very fine anti-Bolshevik film, and "Wings" which is all about aeroplane fighting and perfectly marvellous. I was so much impressed by it that I went a second time. . . .'*

182

Churchill and his son at Dampierre. On 8 April 1928 Churchill wrote to his wife: '*Very satisfactory reports have arrived about Randolph. . . . There is no doubt he is developing fast, and in those directions wh will enable him to make his way in the world – by writing & speaking – in politics, at the bar, or in journalism. There are some vy strange & even formidable traits in his character. His mind is free & growing more powerful every day. It is quite startling to hear him argue. His present phase is rabid Agnosticism, & last night in argument with Grigg he more than defended his dismal position. The logical strength of his mind, the courage of his thought, & the brutal & sometimes repulsive character of his rejoinders impressed me vy forcibly. He is far more advanced than I was at his age, & quite out of the common – for good or ill.*'

184 Churchill on board the giant Short Brothers 'Calcutta' flying boat, moored on the Thames opposite the Houses of Parliament. Throughout his life he retained a keen interest in new inventions and means of transport. In 1924 he had published a pamphlet, entitled 'Shall We Commit Suicide', in which he had asked: *'Have we reached the end? ... May there not be methods of using explosive energy incomparably more intense than anything heretofore discovered? Might not a bomb no bigger than an orange be found to possess a secret power to destroy a whole block of buildings – nay, to concentrate the force of a thousand tons of cordite and blast a township at a stroke? Could not explosives even of the existing type be guided automatically in flying machines by wireless or other rays, without a human pilot, in ceaseless procession upon a hostile city, arsenal, camp, or dockyard?'*

hurchill on his way to deliver his fourth budget, 24 April 1928. With him (in top hat) is his
arliamentary Private Secretary, Robert Boothby. Among the measures which Churchill
troduced was the first British tax on petrol, fixed at fourpence a gallon.

185 Churchill and his daughter Sarah photographed at Chartwell on 3 September 1928, laying the bricks for a new cottage on the estate. Sarah's fourteenth birthday was a month later. On the following day this photograph (minus Sarah) was published in the 'Daily Sketch' with the comment: *'Those who may be inclined to point out that he has not got his coat off should bear in mind that he took it off when he was helping to lay the foundations, and that, anyhow, he is wearing an old suit. He lays one brick a minute.'*

186

Churchill and his wife at 11 Downing Street, after he had driven up from Chartwell on 15 April 1929, to give his fifth budget. Behind them are Randolph, Robert Boothby (in top hat) and Sarah. One of his new measures was to remove the Preferential Duty on tea. Thus tea prices fell in 1929 (on the eve of the election), just as petrol prices had risen in 1928. He also abolished the Betting Tax, ánd reduced Publican's Licences. Before Churchill, only Walpole Pitt, Peel and Gladstone had introduced and carried five consecutive budgets; each was, or was to become, Prime Minister.

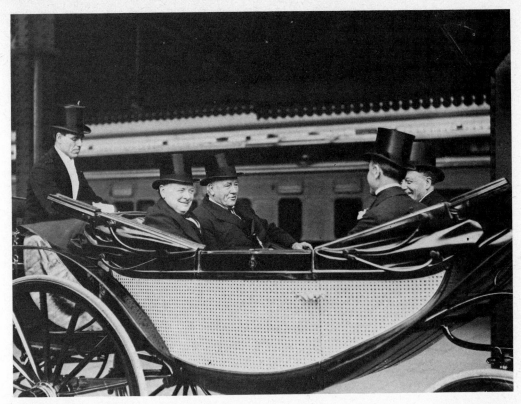

188 The General Election was held on 30 May 1929, and the Labour Party returned to power with more MPs (although less overall votes) than the Conservatives. This photograph shows Churchill and Lord Cushenden (Chancellor of the Duchy of Lancaster) leaving Windsor Station to hand in their seals of office to the King on 7 June.

187

Churchill as Chancellor of the Exchequer: a photograph issued on the front page of his election manifesto, 10 May 1929. In his manifesto Churchill denounced the Socialists who, he wrote, had planned during the General Strike *'to paralyse the life and industry of the whole Island, and if they had succeeded, they would have subverted the representative and parliamentary institutions under which we have lived and grown since the great Civil War of the 17th Century'*. This was a major theme of his election speeches. On 12 February he had told a mass meeting of the 'Anti-Socialist and Anti-Communist Union' in London: *'Socialism today is intellectually bankrupt and discredited, and has been proved on a gigantic scale and with perfect clearness to be fatal to the welfare of living nations. But we have seen with melancholy feelings how year after year a larger number of our own fellow-countrymen have allowed themselves to drift into an easy acceptance of Socialist doctrines, and let themselves be regimented under foreign made standards of Communist collectivism.'*

189 and 190 No longer a Minister, Churchill left England on 3 August 1929 for a three-month visit to Canada and the United States. These photographs were taken at Calgary. With him below are his son Randolph, his nephew John-George, and his brother Jack. On 21 September, while they were in Hollywood, Churchill persuaded Charlie Chaplin to do imitations of Napoleon, Uriah Heep, Henry Irving, and John Barrymore as Hamlet. Randolph Churchill noted in his diary: *'Papa & Charlie sat up till about 3. Papa wants him to act the young Napoleon and has promised to write the Scenario'.*

191
Churchill
returned to
England in
November 1929.
It was ten
years before he
held public
office again.
Much of that
time he spent
writing books:
his memoirs
'My Early Life'
(published in
1930); 'The
World Crisis:
The Eastern
Front' (1931);
'Thoughts and
Adventures'
(1932); a life of
his ancestor
John Duke of
Marlborough
(1933); and
'Great
Contemporaries'
(1937, revised
1938). He did
most of his
writing at
Chartwell, where
this photograph
was taken
during a visit
from Charlie
Chaplin.

192 Churchill and Lloyd George at the Memorial Service for Lord Balfour, Westminster Abbey, 22 March 1930. Writing in the 'Strand' magazine in April 1931 Churchill reflected: '*Arthur Balfour did not mingle in the hurly-burly. He glided upon its surface. . . . His aversion from the Roman Catholic faith was dour and inveterate. Otherwise he seemed to have the personal qualification of a great Pope. . . . When they took him to the Front to see the war, he admired with bland interest through his pince-nez the bursting shells. Luckily none came near enough to make him jump, as they will make any man jump, if they have their chance. . . . [In December 1916] he passed from our Cabinet to the other, from the Prime Minister who was his champion to the Prime Minister who had been his most powerful critic, like a powerful graceful cat walking delicately and unsoiled across a rather muddy street.*'

193

Randolph Churchill about to leave Waterloo station for a lecture tour of the United State Only nineteen years old, he was still an undergraduate at Oxford, and as a result of t tour, never took a university degree. But, as he wrote in his memoirs, 'Twenty-One Years '*The idea of going off to America and teaching, rather than learning, appealed to me strongl and I resolved to go. Everybody except my father thought I was crazy; he encouraged me embark on the venture.*'

FIRST

194 In 1930 Churchill was elected Chancellor of Bristol University. On his first visit to Bristol he was placed *'under arrest'* by the students, who had found him guilty *'of acquiring a new hat and a new chancellorship and with neglecting to supply forenoon coffee and biscuits to the students'*.

195
On 30 October 1930 at a
meeting of Conservative
MPs at Caxton Hall, a
majority voted in favour
of Baldwin's continued
leadership of the Con-
servative Party. But
Churchill had already be-
gun to oppose Baldwin's
policy of eventual self-
government for India,
and on 28 September had
informed the Press that
he would not even con-
sider retiring from public
life while the question of
India's future was still
undecided. On 1 October
he wrote to Lord Burn-
ham: '*I am deeply con-
cerned about the folly and
weakness which is going to
throw India into hideous
confusion.*'

196 Austen Chamberlain (with cigarette and eye glass), Sir Robert Horne and Churchill outside Caxton Hall, 30 October 1930. The meeting marked the beginning of five years' sustained and bitter opposition by Churchill to the Conservative Party's India policy.

Churchill waiting to speak at the first meeting of the Indian Empire Society, at Cannon Street, London on 12 December 1930. During his speech he denounced Conservative Party plans to give India Dominion Status, with the right to secede from the British Empire, telling the audience: *'The extremists who are, and will remain, the dominant force among the Indian political classes have in their turn moved their goal forward to absolute independence, and picture to themselves an early date when they will obtain complete control of the whole of Hindustan, when the British will be no more to them than any other European nation, when white people will be in India only upon sufferance, when debts and obligations of all kinds will be repudiated and when an army of white janissaries, officered if necessary from Germany, will be hired to secure the armed ascendancy of the Hindu. All these absurd and dangerous pretensions have so far been met in speech with nothing but soft deprecatory and placatory words by the British Government in India, or at home. . . . The truth is that Gandhi-ism and all it stands for will, sooner or later, have to be grappled with and finally crushed. It is no use trying to satisfy a tiger by feeding him with cat's-meat. . . . We have no intention of casting away the most truly bright and precious jewel in the crown of the King, which more than all our other Dominions and Dependencies constitutes the glory and strength of the British Empire. The loss of India would mark and consummate the downfall of the British Empire. That great organism would pass at a stroke out of life into history. From such a catastrophe there could be no recovery.'*

198 On 31 December 1931; while on a lecture tour in the United States, Churchill was knocked over by a taxi-cab in New York and badly injured. This photograph shows him leaving the Lennox Hill Hospital, New York.

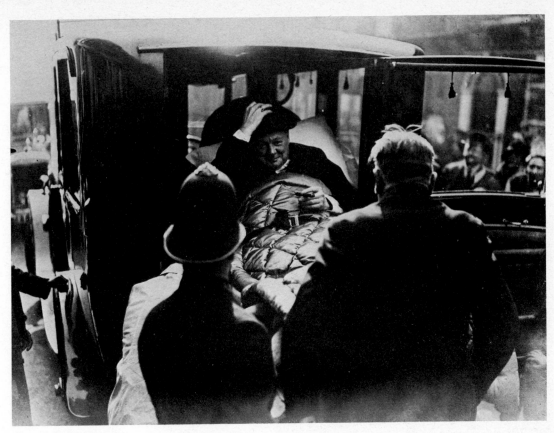

199 On 27 September 1932 Churchill was taken ill with paratyphoid. In this photograph he is seen leaving the Beaumont Street Nursing Home in London on 10 October. For six weeks he recuperated at Chartwell. Then, on 23 November, he returned to the House of Commons, and spoke with foreboding of the future of Europe, of the dangers of premature disarmament, and of the dangers of the Nazi movement: '*Do not delude yourselves. Do not let His Majesty's Government believe – I am sure they do not believe – that all that Germany is asking for is equal status. . . . All these bands of sturdy Teutonic youths, marching through the streets and roads of Germany, with the light of desire in their eyes to suffer for their Fatherland, are not looking for status. They are looking for weapons, and, when they have the weapons, believe me they will then ask for the return of lost territories and lost colonies, and when that demand is made it cannot fail to shake and possibly shatter to their foundations every one of the countries I have mentioned (Belgium, Poland, Rumania, Czechoslovakia and Yugoslavia).*' And Churchill continued: '*. . . I would now say, "Tell the truth to the British people." They are a tough people, a robust people. They may be a bit offended at the moment, but if you have told them exactly what is going on you have insured yourself against complaints and reproaches which are very unpleasant when they come home on the morrow of some disillusion. . . .*' Churchill then spoke of the policy which he believed should be pursued: '*I would follow any real path, not a sham or a blind alley, which led to lasting reconciliation between Germany and her neighbours. . . . Here is my general principle. The removal of the just grievances of the vanquished ought to precede the disarmament of the victors. . . . It would be far safer to reopen questions like those of the Dantzig Corridor and Transylvania, with all their delicacy and difficulty, in cold blood and in a calm atmosphere and while the victor nations still have ample superiority, than to wait and drift on, inch by inch and stage by stage, until once again vast combinations, equally matched, confront each other face to face.*'

Nazi Movement—Local Version

201 Lloyd George and Churchill in November 1934, at the Printers' Pension Corporation Festival Dinner, held at The Connaught Rooms in London. A year earlier, in August 1933, both of them – and also Austen Chamberlain – had been excluded by the BBC from taking part in a series of broadcast political talks. All three had protested about the ban, writing to the Chairman of the BBC, J. H. Whitley, on 23 August 1933: '. . . *we are the three senior Privy Councillors in the House of Commons. . . . Such a principle if applied in Parliament would reduce its debates to mere regimentations of machine-controlled opinion and would deny fair expression to independent and non-official news.*' The protest (which was sent from Chartwell) was in vain; the BBC persisted in its ban.

200

Churchill's continued denunciation of India self-government associated him, for the first time in his life, with the right-wing of the Conservative Party, to whom he appeared as a potential leader, and an alternative to Baldwin. On 30 March 1933 this cartoon appeared in the 'Daily Herald'. That same day Churchill told the House of Commons that: '*He would appeal particularly to the new members. Let them beware that in years to come they did not find themselves sitting by their own fireside when across the dark distances from India, to quote the phrase of John Morley, they would hear "the dull roar and scream of carnage and confusion" coming back to them. Then bitter would be their feelings of responsibility and agony when they felt that they themselves played a part in bringing about a situation of such frightful disaster.*' Of the people of India Churchill said: '*100,000,000 of human beings are here to greet the dawn, to toil upon the plains, to bow before the temples of inexorable gods. Because they are here you cannot abandon them. They are as much our children as any children can be. They are actually in the world as the result of what this nation and this Parliament have done. It is impossible that you should leave them to be diminished by the hideous process of diminution which keeps the population of China in check. It is impossible that you should hand them over to the oppressor and to the spoiler and disinterest yourself in their fortunes. By every law of God or man Parliament is responsible for them, and never could we hold an honourable name among the nations if we pretended that, by any sophistry of liberal doctrine or constitutional theory, we could give away our responsibility, so vital and great.*'

202 A photograph taken at the accession of Edward VIII, on 20 January 1936. Churchill is with a group of Privy Councillors (Sir Herbert Samuel is on the left. Churchill was anxious to return to the Cabinet, from which he had already been excluded for seven years. But on 21 February he wrote to his wife of how the new Prime Minister, Stanley Baldwin, '*desires above all things to avoid bringing me in. This I must now recognize. But his own position is much shaken, and the storm clouds gather.*' Six days later Clementine Churchill replied: '*My darling – I think Baldwin must be mad not to ask you to help him. Perhaps it is a case of "Those whom the Gods wish to Destroy. . . .".*' At the end of April, Churchill's name was much canvassed for the newly created post of Minister for Co-ordination of Defence, but Baldwin refused to bring him back. On 3 March, Churchill wrote to his wife: '*I do not mean to break my heart whatever happens. Destiny plays her part.*' If a post could be found for him, he added, '*I will work faithfully before God and man for PEACE, and not allow pride or excitement to sway my spirit.*'

203 Churchill on board the Admiralty yacht 'Enchantress' at Spithead, May 1936, when the new King, Edward VIII, reviewed the Fleet. Having failed to undermine Baldwin's Indian policy, or to dislodge him from the leadership of the Conservative Party, Churchill took up the new King's cause at the time of the abdication, and protested bitterly against Baldwin's part in the abdication crisis. On 5 December 1936 Churchill issued a public statement: '*I plead for time and patience. The nation must realise the character of the constitutional issue. There is no question of any conflict between the King and Parliament. Parliament has not been consulted in any way, nor allowed to express any opinion. The question is whether the King is to abdicate upon the advice of the Ministers of the day. No such advice has ever before been tendered to a Sovereign in Parliamentary times . . . If the King refuses to take the advice of his Ministers, they are, of course, free to resign. They have no right whatever to put pressure upon him to accept their advice by soliciting beforehand assurances from the Leader of the Opposition that he will not form an alternative administration in the event of their resignation, and thus confronting the King with an ultimatum. . . . Howsoever this matter may turn, it is pregnant with calamity and inseparable from inconvenience. But all the evil aspects will be aggravated beyond measure if the utmost chivalry is not shown, both by Ministers and by the British nation, toward a gifted and beloved King, torn between private and public obligations of love and duty.*' Two days later the House of Commons shouted Churchill down when he pleaded for delay on the King's behalf. Edward VIII abdicated on 9 December. Churchill's political reputation was at a low ebb. '*He has undermined in five minutes the patient reconstruction work of five years*' Harold Nicolson noted in his diary.

204 Churchill and his son after bathing at Chartwell, 1935. Churchill had himself supervised the building of the swimming pool on the estate.

205 Churchill walking in the grounds of Chartwell with his friend Ralph Wigram, a senior Foreign Office official who shared Churchill's fears of Nazi Germany. Wigram died suddenly at the age of forty, on 31 December 1936. On learning of Wigram's death Churchill wrote to Mrs Wigram (later Ava, Viscountess Waverley): '*I admired always so much his courage, integrity of purpose, high comprehending vision. He was one of those – how few – who guard the life of Britain. Now he is gone – and on the eve of this fateful year. Indeed it is a blow to England, and to all the best that England means. It is only a week or so that he rang me up to speak about the late King. I can hear his voice in my memory. And You? What must be your loss? But still you will have a right to dwell on all that you did for him. You shielded that bright steady flame that burned in the broken lamp. But for you it would long ago have been extinguished, and its light would not have guided us thus far upon our journey.*'

207 Churchill and Lord Halifax (the Foreign Secretary) in conversation in Whitehall, 29 March 1938. Hitler had annexed Austria seventeen days earlier, on 21 March. On 14 March, Churchill told the House of Commons: '*Europe is confronted with a programme of aggression, nicely calculated and timed, unfolding stage by stage, and there is only one choice open, not only to us but to other countries, either to submit like Austria, or else take effective measures while time remains to ward off the danger, and if it cannot be warded off to cope with it. . . . If we go on waiting upon events, how much shall we throw away of resources now available for our security and the maintenance of peace? How many friends will be alienated, how many potential allies shall we see go one by one down the grisly gulf? How many times will bluff succeed until behind bluff ever gathering forces have accumulated reality? . . . Where are we going to be two years hence, for instance, when the German Army will certainly be much larger than the French Army, and when all the small nations will have fled from Geneva to pay homage to the everwaxing powers of the Nazi system, and to make the best terms that they can for themselves?*'

206

Churchill at Chartwell, supervising the building of a new cottage on the estate, 25 February 1938. Although he had been out of office for over eight years, Churchill now emerged as the most vociferous advocate of rearmament, and international alliances, within the League of Nations, to deter German or Italian aggression. On 4 February 1938 he had declared, in an article in the 'Evening Standard': '*What is the alternative to the League of Nations and the maintenance of its authority, weakened as it now is? The alternative is sombre. It is for Britain and France, rich, powerful, heavily armed, to stand aside and allow Central and Eastern Europe to clatter into anarchy, or congeal into a Nazi domination. . . . This process would not be pleasant to any of the States now existing in Middle Europe. It would be accompanied by intense internal stresses such as destroyed the empire of the great Napoleon. It would be melancholy for the world. It seems very likely that the Western democracies would remain erect at the end of it. But what a cataract of misfortune would be opened upon these short-sighted governments and unfortunately peoples, who through mere incapacity to combine upon a broad international platform had left themselves the prey to measureless tribulation!*' On 16 February Hitler demanded – and obtained – the inclusion of Austrian Nazis in the Austrian Government.

**208
and
209**

Two photographs of Churchill leaving 10 Downing Street on 10 September 1938, during the Czech crisis. He was bitterly opposed to the Munich agreement signed by Hitler, Neville Chamberlain, Mussolini and Daladier which ceded large areas of Czechoslovakia to Germany. On 5 October he told the House of Commons: '*I do not grudge our loyal, brave people, who were ready to do their duty no matter what cost, who never flinched under the strain of last week – I do not grudge them the natural, spontaneous outburst of joy and relief when they learned that the hard ordeal would no longer be required of them at the moment; but they should know the truth. They should know that there has been gross neglect and deficiency in our defences; they should know that we have sustained a defeat without a war, the consequences of which will travel far with us along our road; they should know that we have passed an awful milestone in our history, when the whole equilibrium of Europe has been deranged, and that the terrible words have for the time being been pronounced against the Western democracies: "Thou art weighed in the balance and found wanting." And do not suppose that this is the end. This is only the beginning of the reckoning. This is only the first sip, the first foretaste of a bitter cup which will be proffered to us year by year unless by a supreme recovery of moral health and martial vigour, we arise again and take our stand for freedom as in the olden time.*'

**210
and
211** On 25 February 1939 the magazine 'Picture Post' sent a photographer to Chartwell, to photograph Churchill at work.

**212
and
213**   In his study at Chartwell, 25 February 1939.

214 Churchill flies as a co-pilot, 16 April 1939, while visiting No 615 Auxiliary Air Force Squadron at Kenley. He had just been gazetted as the Squadron's Honorary Air Commodore. Nine days earlier, Italy had invaded Albania, and on 13 April Churchill had argued in the House of Commons in favour of compulsory national service, and a fuller use of national talent: *'The danger is now very near. A great part of Europe is to a very large extent mobilised. Millions of men are being prepared for war. Everywhere the frontier defences are manned. . . . How can we bear to continue to lead our comfortable, easy life here at home, unwilling even to pronounce the word "compulsion", unwilling even to take the necessary measure by which the armies that we have promised can alone be recruited and equipped? How can we continue – let me say it with particular frankness and sincerity – with less than the full force of the nation incorporated in the governing instrument? These very methods, which the Government owe it to the nation and to themselves to take, are not only indispensable to the duties that we have accepted but, by their very adoption, they may rescue our people and the people of many lands from the dark, bitter waters which are rising fast on every side.'* The House of Commons and the Government accepted Churchill's arguments. On 18 April his friend Brendan Bracken wrote to the American Financier Bernard Baruch: *'Winston has won his long fight. Our Government are now adopting the policy that he advised three years ago. No public man in our time has shown more foresight. And I believe that his long, lonely struggle to expose the dangers of the dictatorships will prove to be the best chapter in his crowded life.'*

215 Churchill addresses a lunch-time crowd at the Mansion House, London, on 24 April 1939, as part of the national drive for Territorial Army recruits. On his right is the Lord Mayor of London, Sir Frank Bowater. On 18 May Parliament passed a Bill for the introduction of compulsory national service. On the following day Churchill told an audience at the Corn Exchange in Cambridge: '*We have every reason to be contented with the reception which the Conscription Bill has received abroad. It could never have been intended to overawe Germany or Italy. In those countries they count their soldiers by the million; and Signor Mussolini says that he has eight million. Therefore the addition of two hundred thousand young men to our armed forces is no menace to the Dictator Powers. It is the effect upon our Allies and those countries to whom we have given guarantees that is important.*'

216 Leon Blum, the French Socialist leader (and former Prime Minister) visited Churchill at Chartwell on 10 May 1939. Nine days later, speaking at the Corn Exchange in Cambridge, Churchill declared, as an argument in favour of Compulsory National Service: *'The French do not easily understand that an island people who have not seen the watch fires of a hostile camp on their own soil for a thousand years have deep prejudices against militarism, and are historically attached to the voluntary system. They only know that they would have to stand for many terrible months against the German Army, and that we were not willing to put our prejudices aside, or depart from our normal system. They would not think it fair, and it would not have been fair.'*

MR. WINSTON CHURCHILL AND MR. ANTHONY EDEN
DEMAND A WHOLE-HEARTED ALLIANCE WITH RUSSIA.

217 During the Spring and Summer of 1939, Churchill was joined in his opposition to Government policy by Anthony Eden (who had resigned as Foreign Secretary in February 1938). Both believed that one way of deterring Hitler from aggression in Europe was by an immediate alliance between Britain, France and the Soviet Union. This cartoon was published in 'Punch' on 31 May 1939. But Neville Chamberlain distrusted Soviet intentions, and on 24 August 1939 the Soviet Union signed a non-aggression pact with Hitler, a secret clause of which envisaged the partition of Poland between Russia and Germany.

CALLING MR. CHURCHILL

218 and 219 Throughout the summer of 1939 there was a growing public demand for Churchill's inclusion in the Government. Strube's cartoon 'Calling Mr Churchill' was published in the 'Daily Express' on 6 July; Shepard's cartoon 'The Old Sea-Dog' appeared in 'Punch' six days later. In Strube's cartoon, Neville Chamberlain is sitting in the arm chair, and three Press Lords, Lord Kemsley, Lord Camrose and Lord Beaverbrook, are (left to right) calling for Churchill. Although he was not invited to join the Government, Churchill continued to speak, to write and to broadcast as a private citizen. On 2 August he warned the House of Commons of an imminent German attack on Poland. '*I may be wrong,*' he said, '*but I have not always been wrong.*' And on 8 August he broadcast to the people of the United States. '*If Herr Hitler does not make war,*' he said, '*there will be no war. No one else is going to make war. Britain and France are determined to shed no blood except in self-defence or in defence of their Allies.*'

THE OLD SEA-DOG

"Any telegram for me?"

220 A giant poster, paid for by an unknown Churchill supporter, which appeared in the Strand on 24 July 1939. Chamberlain refused to bring Churchill into his Government. But the French Government, led by Paul Reynaud, invited him, early in August, to examine the defence works of the Maginot Line.

221 For ten days in August, Churchill visited the French Maginot Line defences as the guest of the French Army. After visiting the Maginot Line, he went for a few days to the Chateau St George Motel, in Normandy – the house of Consuelo Balsan – where he painted and fished.

222

Churchill at St George Motel; this and the previous photograph were both taken on 22 August 1939, by the painter Paul Maze, who later recalled: 'Winston was painting that day. He suddenly turned to me and said *"This is the last picture we shall paint in peace for a very long time. . . ."* As he worked he would now and then make statements as to the strength of the German Army. *"They are strong, I tell you, they are strong,"* he would say. Then his jaw would clench his large cigar, and I felt the determination of his will. *"Ah,"* he would say, *"with it all, we shall have him."* '

223 Churchill returned to England from France on the evening of 23 August 1939. This photograph was taken on his arrival at Croydon airport.

224 In the last week of August, Hitler began to threaten Poland. On 25 August Neville Chamberlain announced that if Poland were invaded, Britain would declare war in her defence. Parliament was summoned four days later on 29 August. Churchill and Eden (both of whom were still excluded from the Government) were photographed in Whitehall walking together to the House of Commons.

225 On 1 September 1939 Hitler invaded Poland. That same day, Chamberlain asked Churchill to join the Cabinet, as First Lord of the Admiralty. On 3 September Britain declared war on Germany. That afternoon Churchill told the House of Commons: '*Outside, the storms of war may blow and the lands may be lashed with the fury of its gales, but in our own hearts this Sunday morning there is peace. Our hands may be active, but our consciences are at rest. . . . This is not a question of fighting for Danzig or fighting for Poland. We are fighting to save the whole world from the pestilence of Nazi tyranny and in defence of all that is most sacred to man. This is no war for domination or imperial aggrandisement or material gain; no war to shut any country out of its sunlight and means of progress. It is a war . . . to establish, on impregnable rocks, the rights of the individual, and it is a war to establish and revive the stature of man.*' This photograph was taken on the morning of 4 September, Churchill's first full day at the Admiralty. His gas mask is with his two despatch boxes.

226 Churchill leaves the Admiralty for a meeting of the War Cabinet at 10 Downing Street on 5 September 1939.

227 Churchill arrives at 10 Downing Street from the Admiralty (in background), on the morning of 18 September 1939, after receiving news of the sinking of the aircraft carrier 'Courageous'. Over five hundred of her crew of 1,260 had been drowned.

228 Churchill making his first wartime broadcast, on 1 October 1939, after the defeat of Poland, and its partition between Hitler and Stalin. During the broadcast he said: '*Poland has been again overrun by two of the great Powers which held her in bondage for 150 years, but were unable to quench the spirit of the Polish nation. The heroic defence of Warsaw shows that the soul of Poland is indestructible, and that she will rise again like a rock, which may for a spell be submerged by a tidal wave, but which remains a rock.*' Later in his broadcast Churchill said: '*I cannot forecast to you the action of Russia. It is a riddle wrapped in a mystery inside an enigma: but perhaps there is a key. That key is Russian national interest. It cannot be in accordance with the interest or the safety of Russia that Germany should plant itself upon the shores of the Black Sea, or that it should overrun the Balkan States and subjugate the Slavonic peoples of South-Eastern Europe. That would be contrary to the historic life-interests of Russia.*'

230 A German cartoon, sent to Churchill at the end of October.

229

Churchill leaving the Admiralty on his way to a meeting of the War Council on 14 October 1939, shortly after learning that the battleship Royal Oak had been sunk while at anchor in Scapa Flow. A month later, on 12 November, he told the House of Commons: '*We do not at all underrate the power and malignity of our enemies. We are prepared to endure tribulation. But we made up our minds about all this ten weeks ago, and everything that has happened since has made us feel that we were right then and are still right now. No one in the British Islands supposed this was going to be a short or easy war. Nothing has ever impressed me so much as the calm, steady, businesslike resolution with which the masses of our wage-earning folk and ordinary people in our great cities faced what they imagined would be a fearful storm about to fall on them and their families at the very first moment. They all prepared themselves to have the worst happen to them at once, and they braced themselves for the ordeal. They did not see what else there was to do.*'

231 On 5 November 1939 Churchill visited Paris to discuss Anglo-French naval activity with the French Minister of Marine. While in Paris, several French Ministers spoke to him despondently of the war. General Spears, who was present, heard Churchill remark to one of them: '*We are quite capable of beating the Germans singlehanded.*' On his way back to England, Churchill visited the Commander-in-Chief of the British Expeditionary Force, Lord Gort, at his headquarters in France (the Chateau de Courcy, near Avesnes). Here he is seen with Gort, and the Chief of the General Staff, Lieutenant-General Pownall (who is filling his pipe). Churchill's aide-de-camp, Commander C. R. 'Tommy' Thompson can be seen reflected in the mirror. Thompson accompanied Churchill on nearly all his wartime journeys.

Lord Gort and Churchill at Avesnes, 5 November 1939

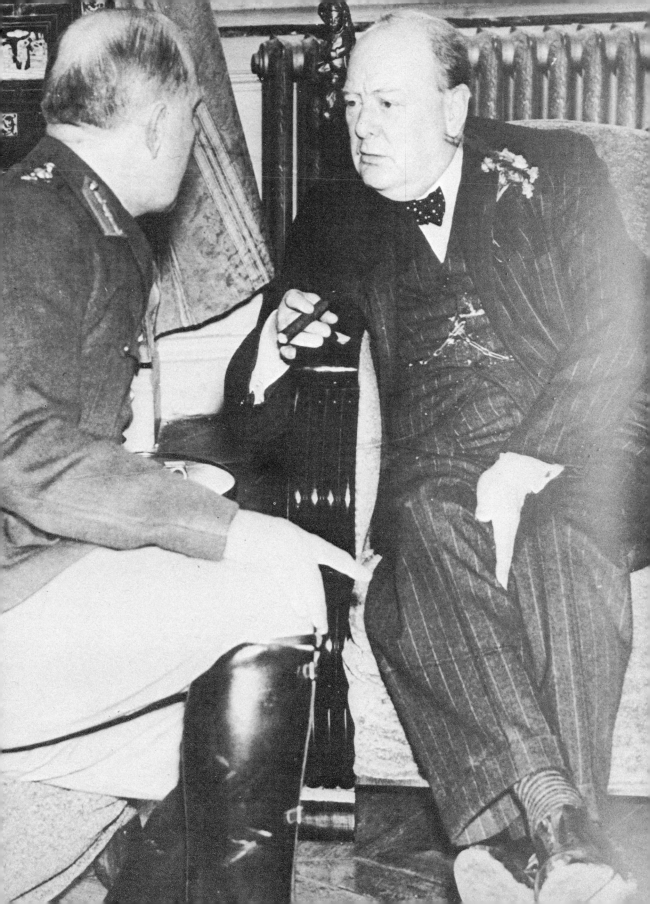

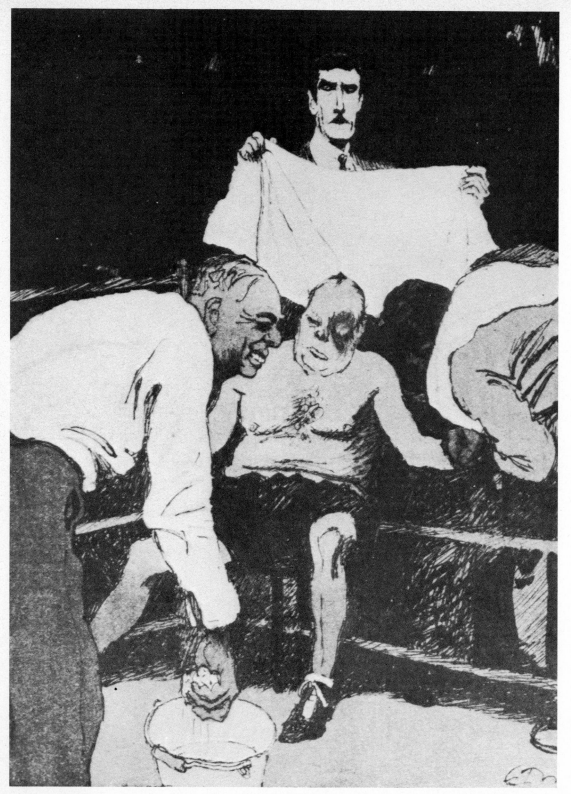

233 A German cartoon, published in 'Simplicissimus' (Munich) on 5 November 1939. Anthony Eden (who had returned as Secretary of State for the Dominions, but was not in the War Cabinet) is holding the towel; Leslie Hore-Belisha (Secretary of State for War) is wetting the sponge. The caption read: '*Churchill received several hard body-blows. Undoubtedly we have won the first round.*'

234 A photograph of the War Cabinet taken on 8 November 1939. In the front row are: Lord Halifax (Foreign Secretary), Sir John Simon (Chancellor of the Exchequer), Neville Chamberlain (Prime Minister), Sir Samuel Hoare (Lord Privy Seal), and Lord Chatfield (Minister for Co-ordination of Defence). Standing are Sir Kingsley Wood (Secretary of State for Air), Churchill, Leslie Hore-Belisha (Secretary of State for War) and Lord Hankey (Minister without Portfolio). The portrait on the wall is of the 3rd Marquess of Salisbury (Prime Minister at the time of the Boer War).

"Himmel! It's That Man Again"

235 A cartoon published in the 'Evening News' on 13 November 1939. On the previous day Churchill had told the House of Commons: '*The whole world is against Hitler and Hitlerism. Men of every race and clime feel that this monstrous apparition stands between them and the forward move which is their due, and for which the age is ripe. Even in Germany itself there are millions who stand aloof from the seething mass of criminality and corruption constituted by the Nazi Party machine. Let them take courage amid perplexities and perils, for it may well be that the final extinction of a baleful domination will pave the way to a broader solidarity of all the men in all the lands than we could ever have planned if we had not marched together through the fire.*'

236

Churchill at a meeting of the Admirality Board on 17 November 1939. In a series of Minutes he exorted his staff to action and vigilance. On 12 December he minuted: '*In view of the danger of surprise attacks at a time when the enemy may expect to find us off our ground, there must be no break or holiday period at Christmas or the New Year. The utmost vigilance must be practised at the Admiralty and in all naval ports.*'

237 On 14 February 1940 Churchill went to Plymouth to welcome the cruiser 'Exeter' on her return from sinking the Nazi pocket battleship 'Admiral Graf Spee' at the battle of the River Plate. Sixty of the 'Exeter's' officers and men had been killed in the action. The ship herself was finally sunk by the Japanese in the battle of the Straits of Sunda in 1942.

238 Churchill cheered by the officers and men of the 'Exeter'.

239 Churchill at the Guildhall, 23 February 1940, when the survivors of the 'Exeter' were given a lunch by the King and Queen. Neville Chamberlain is standing just behind Churchill (in top hat). Speaking at the luncheon, Churchill declared: '. . . *although mistakes and accidents will certainly occur, and sorrow will fall from time to time upon us, we hope that from Whitehall the sense of resolution and design at the centre will impart itself to all afloat, and will lighten the burden of their task and concert the vigour of their action.*'

240 On 28 March 1940 the Franco-British Supreme War Council met in London. Churchill was photographed leaving the luncheon in happy mood. The Council – at which Neville Chamberlain and Paul Reynaud were the principal speakers – decided to deprive Germany of Swedish iron ore by laying minefields along the Norwegian coast (inside Norwegian territorial waters) where the ore had to pass, and thus force the German ore ships into the open sea, where they could be hunted down.

241

Churchill photographed leaving the Admiralty – and knocking the ash off his cigar – on the morning of 4 April 1940, just after it had been announced that, while remaining First Lord of the Admiralty, he was also to be the head of a Committee made up of the three Service Ministers and the Army, Navy and Air Force Chiefs of Staff. Neville Chamberlain had instructed Churchill's Committee to make regular recommendations to the War Cabinet on the general conduct of the war. Commenting on this development, the Associated Press wrote: *'The new appointment, in fact, makes Mr Churchill the country's war chief.'*

242 Churchill was a leading advocate of British military and naval action to deprive Germany of Swedish iron ore. But the British minelaying along the Norwegian coast came too late; Hitler forestalled it by sending German troops into Denmark and Norway, and by the first week of May 1940 the position of the British forces – who had landed at several Norwegian ports, was precarious. This photograph shows Churchill in Horse Guards parade on the morning of 7 May 1940, about to enter the garden door of 10 Downing Street. That afternoon the House of Commons began to debate the efficiency of Chamberlain's conduct of the war, and the Norwegian expedition. Churchill sought to defend Chamberlain's policy, and the Navy's part in it, but over 80 Conservative MPs opposed the Government, thus challenging Chamberlain's leadership.

**243
and
244** Shaken by the severe criticisms of the Norwegian debate, Chamberlain decided to form a Coalition Government. But before he could do this, Hitler invaded France, Belgium, Holland and Luxemburg. This new danger was discussed by the Cabinet on the morning of 10 May 1940. These photographs show Sir Kingsley Wood, Churchill and Anthony Eden leaving the Cabinet meeting. Churchill's personal detective, Inspector Thompson, can be seen in the doorway, behind Eden.

245 Because of the German invasion of France, Belgium, Holland and Luxemburg, Neville Chamberlain decided that he must form an all-Party Government. But the Labour Party, led by Clement Attlee, refused to serve under him. During 10 May 1940 Chamberlain asked Lord Halifax if he was willing to try to form a Coalition, but Halifax declined. He then asked Churchill, who accepted. That same day Churchill became Prime Minister. In his memoirs he recalled: '. . . *as I went to bed at about 3 a.m., I was conscious of a profound sense of relief. At last I had the authority to give directions over the whole scene. I felt as if I were walking with destiny, and that all my past life had been but a preparation for this hour and for this trial.*' This photograph shows Churchill leaving the Admiralty for Buckingham Palace on 12 May to see the King, and to attend a meeting of the Privy Council at which the members of his Coalition took their oaths of office.

TWO-GUN WINSTON

246 As well as becoming Prime Minister, Churchill appointed himself Minister of Defence. This cartoon was published in the 'Daily Mail' on 13 May 1940.

247 Churchill crossing Horse Guards Parade on 20 May 1940, the morning after his first broadcast as Prime Minister. During his broadcast he had said: '*I speak to you for the first time as Prime Minister in a solemn hour for the life of our country, of our Empire, of our Allies, and, above all, of the cause of Freedom. . . . This is one of the most awe-striking periods in the long history of France and Britain. It is also beyond doubt the most sublime. Side by side, unaided except by their kith and kin in the great Dominions and by the wide Empires which rest beneath their shield – side by side, the British and French peoples have advanced to rescue not only Europe but mankind from the foulest and most soul-destroying tyranny which has ever darkened and stained the pages of history. Behind them – behind us – behind the Armies and Fleets of Britain and France – gather a group of shattered States and bludgeoned races: the Czechs, the Poles, the Norwegians, the Danes, the Dutch, the Belgians – upon all of whom the long night of barbarism will descend, unbroken even by a star of hope, unless we conquer, as conquer we must, as conquer we shall.*'

249 Churchill and his wife arriving at Westminster Abbey on Sunday 26 May 1940, for National Prayers. Churchill is carrying his gas-mask.

250
Mrs Churchill at 10 Downing Street. This photograph was taken in September 1940.

251 and 252 During May and June of 1940 the Germans overran France, Belgium, Holland and Luxemburg. On 17 June France sued for peace. During August the Germans began to bomb London and the Channel ports, hoping to demoralize the British into asking for peace. Churchill urged defiance, and opposed all talk of surrender. On 28 August he visited Ramsgate. While in the town a German air raid began. These two photographs show Churchill on his way to the air raid shelter in the town's tunnels, and sitting in the shelter. In the top photograph, Inspector Thompson is carrying Churchill's gas mask, as well as his own.

253 The German air raids on London intensified at the beginning of September. Here Churchill is seen visiting bombed and fire-gutted buildings on 8 September. Three days later, on 11 September, he broadcast to the nation, speaking defiantly of *a people who will not flinch or weary of the struggle – hard and protracted though it will be*.

254 and 255 Churchill inspecting bomb damage in the City of London and at Battersea (above) on 10 September 1940. In his radio broadcast on the following day he declared: '*These cruel, wanton, indiscriminate bombings of London are, of course, a part of Hitler's invasion plans. He hopes, by killing large numbers of civilians, and women and children, that he will terrorize and cow the people of this mighty imperial city, and make them a burden and an anxiety to the Government and thus distract our attention unduly from the ferocious onslaught he is preparing. Little does he know the spirit of the British nation, or the tough fibre of the Londoners, whose forebears played a leading part in the establishment of Parliamentary institutions and who have been bred to value freedom far above their lives. This wicked man, the repository and embodiment of many forms of soul-destroying hatred, this monstrous product of former wrongs and shame, has now resolved to try to break our famous Island race by a process of indiscriminate slaughter and destruction. What he has done is to kindle a fire in British hearts, here and all over the world, which will glow long after all traces of the conflagration he has caused in London have been removed. He has lighted a fire which will burn with a steady and consuming flame until the last vestiges of Nazi tyranny have been burnt out of Europe, and until the Old World – and the New – can join hands to rebuild the temples of man's freedom and man's honour, upon foundations which will not soon or easily be overthrown.*'

256 On 3 October 1940 Churchill reconstructed his War Cabinet. Here he is seen leaving 10 Downing Street on the following day with the three Labour members: Ernest Bevin (Minister of Labour), Clement Attlee (Lord Privy Seal), and Arthur Greenwood (Minister without Portfolio). The other members of his new War Cabinet were: Sir John Anderson (President of the Council), Lord Halifax (Foreign Secretary) and Sir Kingsley Wood (Chancellor of the Exchequer).

258 Churchill's own office and bedroom in the underground War Room. Several of his wartime broadcasts were made from this desk. The map at the foot of his bed (normally covered by a curtain) showed in detail the defences of Britain in 1940 and 1941, when invasion seemed imminent.

257 Before the outbreak of war, a Cabinet War Room had been established underground in Whitehall. Here, on 3 September 1939, Neville Chamberlain made his first broadcast after war was declared on Germany, and here, during air raids, and air raid alerts, Churchill conferred with his Cabinet, his War Cabinet, and his Chiefs of Staff.

259 to 261 Churchill and his wife visit the bomb damaged City of London on 31 December 1940. With them (with glasses, and no hat in the bottom left photograph) is the Minister of Information Churchill's friend Brendan Bracken. Later that day Churchill wrote to President Roosevelt: *'They burned a large part of the City of London last night, and the scenes of widespread destruction here and in our provincial centres are shocking; but when I visited the still-burning ruins to-day the spirit of the Londoners was as high as in the first days of the indiscriminate bombing in September, four months ago.'*

262 Churchill watches the first American-built aeroplane arriving in Britain, as part of the Lend–Lease programme instituted by President Roosevelt. The Lend–Lease Act became law on 11 March 1941. Under it, Britain could 'loan' vital war materials for as long as the war might last. Through Lend–Lease, Britain was soon able to replenish her dwindling stocks of food, machine tools and even tobacco. By the end of the war the United States had provided Britain with half its tanks, most of its transport aircraft, a quarter of its ammunition and almost all its extra shipping. Churchill called Lend–Lease '*the most unsordid act in the history of any nation*'. On 22 June 1941 Hitler invaded the Soviet Union; from that moment, at Churchill's insistence, Britain herself sent what aid she could to Russia, despite her own grave shortages.

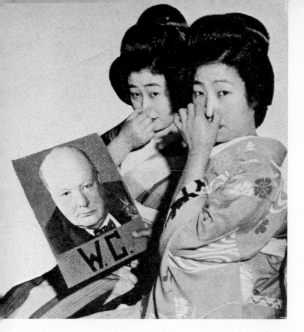

263

Although Japan remained neutral throughout 1940 and most of 1941, her troops continued their conquest of China and Indo-China. This Japanese cartoon, published early in 1941, expressed the official Japanese view.

264
Churchill at Bristol, 14 April 1941, two days after a heavy air raid on the city.

265 and 266 On the morning of 14 July 1941 Churchill reviewed the Civil Defence Services in Hyde Park. After the review, he lunched at County Hall, London and spoke on the progress of the war. During the course of his speech he declared: '*We live in a terrible epoch of the human story, but we believe there is a broad and sure justice running through its theme. It is time that the Germans should be made to suffer in their own homeland and cities something of the torment they have twice in our lifetime let loose upon their neighbours and upon the world. We have now intensified for a month past our systematic, scientific, methodical bombing on a large scale of the German cities, seaports, industries, and other military objectives. We believe it to be in our power to keep this process going, on a steadily rising tide, month after month, year after year, until the Nazi regime is either extirpated by us, or better still, torn to pieces by the German people themselves.*'

267
and
268

At the end of his speech on 14 July 1941 Churchill said: '*We do not expect to hit without being hit back, and we intend with every week that passes to hit harder. Prepare yourselves, then, my friends and comrades in the Battle of London, for this renewal of your exertions. We shall never turn from our purpose, however sombre the road, however grievous the cost, because we know that out of this time of trial and tribulation will be born a new freedom and glory for all mankind.*'

**269
and
270** Churchill inspecting Czechoslovak forces in England, August 1941. In the bottom photograph, President Beneš is on the left.

271 Churchill, photographed during his luncheon with the exiled Czechoslovak leaders, August 1941.

273 On Sunday 10 August Roosevelt joined Churchill on board the 'Prince of Wales' for Divine Service. Later Churchill recalled: *'This service was felt by us all to be a deeply moving expression of the unity of faith of our two peoples, and none who took part in it will forget the spectacle presented that sunlit morning on the crowded quarterdeck – the symbolism of the Union Jack and the Stars and Stripes draped side by side on the pulpit; the American and British chaplains sharing in the reading of the prayers; the highest naval, military, and air officers of Britain and the United States grouped in one body behind the President and me; the close-packed ranks of British and American sailors, completely intermingled, sharing the same books and joining fervently together in the prayers and hymns familiar to both. I chose the hymns myself – "For Those in Peril on the Sea" and "Onward, Christian Soldiers". We ended with "O God, Our Help in Ages Past", which Macaulay reminds us the Ironsides had chanted as they bore John Hampden's body to the grave. Every word seemed to stir the heart. It was a great hour to live. Nearly half those who sang were soon to die.'*

272
On 9 August 1941, while the United States was still neutral, Churchill met Roosevelt on board the 'Augusta' in Placentia Bay, Newfoundland. It was their first wartime meeting. In this photograph, Roosevelt is being supported by his son Elliott; Churchill is handing Roosevelt a letter from King George V. During their meeting, Churchill and Roosevelt discussed the whole future conduct of the war.

274 On board the 'Prince of Wales', August 1941.

275 Churchill with the senior Service advisers who accompanied him on board the 'Prince of Wales'. From left to right: the First Sea Lord, Admiral Pound; the Chief of the Imperial General Staff, General Dill; Churchill; and the Vice-Chief of the Air Staff, Air Marshal Freeman.

276

Churchill with Lord Beaverbrook, on board the 'Prince of Wales'. Beaverbrook had been Minister of Aircraft Production in August 1940, during the Battle of Britain. Later Churchill wrote of him: '*All his remarkable qualities fitted the need. His personal buoyancy and vigour were a tonic. I was glad to be able sometimes to lean on him. He did not fail. . . . His personal force and genius, combined with so much persuasion and contrivance, swept aside many obstacles.*'

277
In Iceland, on his way back to Britain.

278

A photograph of Churchill having tea in a Royal Air Force mess, 25 September 1941. Over a year before, on 20 August 1940, he had told the House of Commons and later, in a broadcast, the whole nation: '*The gratitude of every home in our Island, in our Empire, and indeed throughout the world, except in the abodes of the guilty, goes out to the British airmen who, undaunted by odds, unwearied in their constant challenge and mortal danger, are turning the tide of the world war by their prowess and by their devotion. Never in the field of human conflict was so much owed by so many to so few.*'

279

Churchill at an aeroplane factory in Birmingham, 28 September 1941, watching a girl rivetter at work on a Spitfire. Two days later he told the House of Commons: '*Only the most strenuous exertions, a perfect unity of purpose, added to our traditional unrelenting tenacity, will enable us to act our part worthily in the prodigious world drama in which we are now plunged. Let us make sure these virtues are forthcoming.*'

280 Three days later, on 28 September, Churchill spoke to dock labourers while they were having their lunch. According to the official caption issued at the time he asked them: '*Are you managing to get plenty of food?*' to which they replied: '*Aye sir! we are doing grand, thank you.*'

281 Churchill arriving at the back door of 10 Downing Street on the morning of 8 December 1941, after learning that Japanese forces had attacked United States, British and Dutch territory in Asia and the Pacific. The war had become a 'World War', and the United States had become Britain's ally. In his memoirs Churchill recalled: '*No American will think it wrong of me if I proclaim that to have the United States at our side was to me the greatest joy. I could not foretell the course of events. I do not pretend to have measured accurately the martial might of Japan, but now at this very moment I knew the United States was in the war, up to the neck and in to the death. So we had won after all! . . . We had won the war. England would live; Britain would live; the Commonwealth of Nations and the Empire would live. How long the war would last or in what fashion it would end no man could tell, nor did I at this moment care. Once again in our long Island history we should emerge, however, mauled or mutilated, safe and victorious. We should not be wiped out. Our history would not come to an end. We might not even have to die as individuals. Hitler's fate was sealed. Mussolini's fate was sealed. As for the Japanese, they would be ground to powder. All the rest was merely the proper application of overwhelming force.*'

282 The Soviet Ambassador Ivan Maisky, Anthony Eden, the Soviet Foreign Minister, Vyaches-
lav Molotov, Churchill, and Commander Thompson walking in the garden of 10 Downing
Street, after the signature of the Anglo-Soviet Treaty, 26 May 1942. During his visit,
Molotov urged Churchill to open a 'second front' against Hitler in 1942. But Churchill
warned Molotov that Britain would have to have much greater air power before she could
launch a cross-Channel invasion.

283 On the evening of 10 August 1942 Churchill set off from Cairo to Moscow by air to tell Stalin in person that there could be no 'Second Front' in 1942. This photograph shows him on arrival at Moscow airport, on the morning of 13 August, listening to the band playing the Soviet national anthem. In his memoirs he wrote of his feelings on reaching Russia: '*I pondered on my mission to this sullen, sinister Bolshevik State I had once tried so hard to strangle at its birth, and which, until Hitler appeared, I had regarded as the mortal foe of civilised freedom. . . . We had always hated their wicked regime, and, till the German flail beat upon them, they would have watched us being swept out of existence with indifference and glee-fully divided with Hitler our Empire in the East.*'

284 Churchill and Stalin in the Kremlin at a banquet given in Churchill's honour on 16 August 1942. Stalin signed this photograph for Churchill. After his initial, fierce anger at the postponement of a Second Front in Europe, Stalin showed a keen interest in the Anglo-American plans to drive the Germans out of North Africa.

On 20 August Churchill visited the desert front west of Cairo, seven days after General Montgomery had taken command of the Eighth Army. On the following day he telegraphed to the War Cabinet: '. . . *I am satisfied that we have lively, confident, resolute men in command, working together as an admirable team under leaders of the highest military quality. Everything has been done and is being done that is possible, and it is now my duty to return home, as I have no part to play in the battle, which must be left to those in whom we place our trust.*'

Churchill in Cairo, after his visit to Moscow in August 1942. From Cairo, he urged his War Cabinet colleagues to do their utmost to help Russia in every possible way, telegraphing on 19 August: '*Everybody always finds it convenient to ease themselves at the expense of Russia, but grave issues depend upon preserving a good relationship with this tremendous army, now under dire distress.*'

287
On 13 January 1943 Churchill flew to North Africa from London, for further discussions with President Roosevelt and the British and American Chiefs of Staff. Churchill stayed in a hotel at Anfa, a suburb of Casablanca; here he is seen leaving his hotel with his Private Secretary, John Martin (carrying coat), Commander Thompson, Inspector Thompson, and his son Randolph, who was then serving as a Captain on the Tunisian front (and later parachuted into Yugoslavia as a member of the British Military Mission which served with Tito and his partisans behind the German lines).

288 General Giraud, Roosevelt, General de Gaulle and Churchill at Casablanca 24 January 1943, when Churchill and Roosevelt tried in vain to bring about a reconciliation between the two rival French leaders. In his memoirs Churchill recalled: '. . . *we forced them to shake hands in public before all the reporters and photographers. They did so, and the pictures of this event cannot be viewed even in the setting of these tragic times without a laugh.*'

289 Churchill with the Turkish President, Ismet Inönü, at Adana (in southern Turkey), 30 January 1943. Churchill handed Inönü a letter, at the end of which he wrote: '*I have not been in Turkey since 1909, when I met many of the brave men who laid the foundations of the modern Turkey. There is a long story of the friendly relations between Great Britain and Turkey. Across it is a terrible slash of the last war, when German intrigues and British and Turkish mistakes led to our being on opposite sides. We fought as brave and honourable opponents. But those days are done, and we and our American Allies are prepared to make vigorous exertions in order that we shall all be together and continue together to move forward into a world arrangement in which peaceful peoples will have a right to be let alone and in which all peoples will have a chance to help one another.*' Churchill tried to persuade Inönü to enter the war at once, as Britain's ally. But Turkey remained neutral until January 1945.

290 'Commando', the aeroplane in which Churchill had flown both to Russia and to Turkey. As a memento of these flights the aeroplane carried both the Hammer and Sickle, and the Crescent emblems. On 7 February 1943 Churchill flew in 'Commando' from North Africa to England. It was his last flight in her; later, with a different pilot and crew, she crashed with the loss of all on board.

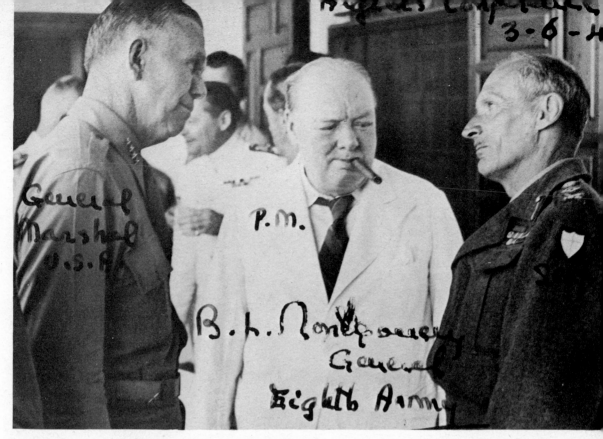

(handwritten annotations on photograph)

Algiers Conference
3·6·4[3]

General Marshall U.S.A.

P.M.

B. L. Montgomery
General
Eighth Army

292 While in Algiers, Churchill finalised the plans for the invasion of Sicily and Italy with the British and American military leaders. This photograph, taken on 3 June 1943, was annotated by General Montgomery, who later recalled: '*Winston wanted me to say the Sicilian invasion would be all right. But I wouldn't.*' But it did in fact succeed. General George Marshall, the Chairman of the American Joint Chiefs of Staff Committee, is on the left.

91 On 11 May 1943 Churchill arrived in the United States for talks with Roosevelt; on 26 May he flew from the United States back to North Africa. Here he is seen in the Roman theatre at Carthage on 1 June, when he was given an ovation by the troops. With him is Lieutenant-General Anderson. In his memoirs Churchill recalled: '*The sense of victory was in the air. The whole of North Africa was cleared of the enemy. A quarter of a million prisoners were cooped in our cages. Everyone was very proud and delighted. There is no doubt that people like winning very much. I addressed many thousand soldiers at Carthage in the ruins of an immense amphitheatre. Certainly the hour and the setting lent themselves to oratory. I have no idea what I said, but the whole audience clapped and cheered as doubtless their predecessors of two thousand years ago had done as they watched gladiatorial combats.*'

MML CONNECTOR

293 Churchill returned to Britain in June 1943. On 9 August he arrived by sea in Canada for a conference at Quebec with Roosevelt, and the Allied Chiefs of Staff, at which the cross-Channel invasion was planned for May 1944. Here, during a journey to the Niagara Falls before the conference opened, Churchill stands at the rear of the train with his daughter Mary (and the ubiquitous Inspector Thompson). At the end of the conference, on 25 August, Churchill telegraphed to the War Cabinet: '*I am feeling rather tired, as the work of the Conference has been very heavy and many large and difficult questions have weighed upon us. I hope my colleagues will think it proper for me to take two or three days' rest. . . .*'

294
British mastery of the air was an indispensable part of the invasion plan. In this photograph, Churchill is seen with his friend Sir Archibald Sinclair (Secretary of State for Air), watching a flying demonstration.

295
Churchill travelling by train, dictating to a secretary.

296 On 27 November 1943 Churchill and Roosevelt went to Teheran for a discussion of war strategy with Stalin. The first meeting was held on 28 November. That night, at dinner, Churchill told Stalin: '*We are the trustees for the peace of the world. If we fail there will be perhaps a hundred years of chaos. . . . There is more than merely keeping the peace. The three Powers should guide the future of the world. I do not want to enforce any system on other nations. I ask for freedom and for the right of all nations to develop as they like.*'

297 On 30 November, while at Teheran, Churchill celebrated his sixty-ninth birthday. In this photograph, Stalin toasts Churchill. Eden is on Churchill's right; Marshal Voroshilov on his left; Churchill's daughter Sarah just behind Stalin; and Averell Harriman (Roosevelt's personal emissary to both Churchill and Stalin) on the far right (lighting a cigarette). During the course of the discussions at Teheran, Stalin suggested shooting 50,000 German officers and technicians as soon as the war was over. But Churchill declared: '*The British Parliament and public will never tolerate mass executions. Even if in war passion they allowed them to begin they would turn violently against those responsible after the first butchery had taken place. . . . I would rather be taken out into the garden here and now and be shot myself than sully my own and my country's honour by such infamy.*'

300 Although not fully recovered from his illness, and against the advice of his doctors, Churchill insisted on returning to Britain. On 14 January 1944 he flew from Marrakesh to Gibraltar, and on the following day sailed for Plymouth on board the battleship 'King George V'. Here he is seen on the bridge, with his daughter Sarah.

Exhausted by his work and travels, Churchill reached Tunis on 12 December 1943. To General Eisenhower, who met him at the airport, he said; '*I am afraid I shall have to stay with you a little longer than I had planned. I am completely at the end of my tether. . . .*' Churchill had contracted pneumonia. Later he recalled: '*The days passed in much discomfort. Fever flickered in and out. . . . The doctors tried to keep the work away from my bedside, but I defied them.*' These photographs show Churchill at Carthage on Christmas Day 1943, above with Generals Eisenhower and Alexander. Two days later he was flown from Tunis to Marrakesh, to recuperate fully from his illness. On the following day he telegraphed to Roosevelt: '*After travelling quite unaffected at 13,000 feet I arrived yesterday at our villa, when I am indeed in the lap of luxury, thanks to overflowing American hospitality. . . . I propose to stay here in the sunshine until I am quite strong again.*' While at Marrakesh, Churchill continued to press forward with plans for the cross-Channel invasion. But his illness was a serious one, and recuperation slow, as he himself later recorded: '*All my painting tackle had been sent out, but I could not face it. I could hardly walk at all. Even tottering from the motor-car to a picnic luncheon in lovely weather amid the foothills of the Atlas was limited to eighty or a hundred yards. I passed eighteen hours out of the twenty-four prone. I never remember such extreme fatigue and weakness in body. . . . I was utterly tired out.*'

301 and 302 Churchill and Eisenhower inspect United States machine gun squadrons 'somewhere in England', during the preparations for the cross-Channel invasion. Eisenhower had been appointed Supreme Commander-in-Chief of the Allied Expeditionary Force. All southern England, Churchill later recalled, '*became a vast military camp, filled with men, trained, instructed, and eager to come to grips with the Germans across the water*'.

303 On 5 June 1944 the Allied Armies in Italy entered Rome. On the following day, 6 June, the Allied Expeditionary Force landed in Normandy. The invasion of northern Europe had begun. This photograph shows Churchill leaving 10 Downing Street on the morning of the invasion. At midday he told the House of Commons: '*Nothing that equipment, science, or forethought could do has been neglected. . . .*' and to Stalin he telegraphed that afternoon: '*Everything has started well. The mines, obstacles, and land batteries have been largely overcome. . . . Infantry landings are proceeding rapidly, and many tanks and self-propelled guns are already ashore.*'

304 On 12 June 1944, six days after the Normandy landings, Churchill crossed to Normandy on the destroyer 'Kelvin'. While he was on board, the destroyer's guns bombed German positions inland. Here, Churchill is seen discussing with Commander 'Tommy' Thompson a suggestion made by General Montgomery (bottom right) as to how best to get out of the landing craft. The Chief of the Imperial General Staff, Sir Alan Brooke, watches (far left, in coat).

305
The dilemma solved, Churchill drives inland in a jeep, accompanied by General Montgomery. He was welcomed by troops unloading and guarding stores, and remained on French soil for seven hours.

306 On 10 July 1944 British troops entered Caen, the first German-held town of size and importance. Twelve days later, on 22 July, Churchill made his third visit to Normandy. Here he is seen, watching German planes being chased by British fighters. From left to right: Lieutenant-General O'Connor (commanding the 8th Corps), Churchill, Field Marshal Smuts, Montgomery and General Brooke.

307 Near Caen, on 22 July, Churchill talked to some of the troops who led the D-Day assault General Montgomery is on the right (in sweater). Recalling his two-day visit to the battle zone, Churchill wrote in his memoirs: '*The nights were very noisy, there being repeated raids by single aircraft, and more numerous alarms. By day I studied the whole process of the landing of supplies and troops, both at the piers, in which I had so long been interested, and on the beaches. On one occasion six tank landing-craft came to the beach in line. When their prows grounded their drawbridges fell forward and out came the tanks, three or four from each, and splashed ashore. In less than eight minutes by my stop-watch the tanks stood in column of route on the highroad ready to move into action. This was an impressive performance, and typical of the rate of discharge which had now been achieved. I was fascinated to see the D.U.K.W.s swimming through the harbour, waddling ashore, and then hurrying up the hill to the great dump where the lorries were waiting to take their supplies to the various units. Upon the wonderful efficiency of this system, now yielding results far greater than we had ever planned, depended the hopes of a speedy and victorious action.*'

308 Churchill at Caen, surveying the ruins; a photograph from General Montgomery's albums. General Dempsey (Commanding the Second Army) is standing between Churchill and Montgomery.

309 On 7 August 1944, during his third visit to Normandy, Churchill relaxes for a moment with one of Montgomery's dogs, 'Rommel'. His other dog was called 'Hitler'; both had been flown over from Portsmouth a short while before. Churchill has changed from his Naval to his Air Commodore's uniform.

310 General Alexander planned a major offensive north of Rome on 26 August 1944. Five days earlier, Churchill himself flew to Rome, for talks with the Italian leaders who – after Mussolini's flight to Northern Italy – had made peace with the Allies. On 23 August he was received by Pope Pius XII, recording in his memoirs: '*We had no lack of topics for conversation. The one that bulked the largest at this audience, as it had done with his predecessor eighteen years before, was the danger of Communism. I have always had the greatest dislike of it....*' On 24 August Churchill flew to Alexander's headquarters at Siena. Here he is seen chatting to troops of the 66th Medium Regiment.

311 On 26 August Churchill flew from Siena to the battle headquarters of the Eighth Army, behind Monte Maggiore. At nine in the morning, only six hours after the attack had been launched, he and Alexander moved forward into the battle zone. This village street had been under German shell fire less than twenty minutes before Churchill arrived.

**312
and
313**

During the morning of 26 August 1944, Churchill reached the ruins of an old castle high above the front line. Watched by the Italian peasant who was living in a nearby hut, he watched the continuing battle. In his memoirs he recorded: '*The Germans were firing with rifles and machine-guns from thick scrub on the farther side of the valley, about five hundred yards away. Our front line was beneath us. The firing was desultory and intermittent. But this was the nearest I got to the enemy and the time I heard most bullets in the Second World War. After about half an hour we went back to our motor-cars and made our way to the river, keeping very carefully to our own wheel tracks or those of other vehicles. At the river we met the supporting columns of infantry, marching up to lend weight to our thin skirmish line, and by five o'clock we were home again at General Leese's headquarters, where the news from the whole of the Army front was marked punctually on the maps.*'

314 General Leese, Churchill and Alexander study the course of the battle, 26 August 1944.

315 Alexander and Churchill confer with Lieutenant-General Anders, the Commander-in-Chief of the Polish forces in Italy. The truck (with its right-hand drive and Arabic markings) had come from Egypt; the armchair from Italy; and the tent (with its swastika emblem, top right) had been captured from the Germans. Throughout 1944 Churchill tried to persuade the exiled Polish leaders and generals to accept eventual Russian control of eastern Poland, with territorial compensation for Poland in the west, from Germany. But the Poles were fearful of trusting Russia, or of making concessions to her. On 14 October Churchill told the Polish Prime Minister in exile, Mikolajczyk: '*I talked to General Anders the other day to whom I took a great liking. He entertains the hope that after the defeat of Germany the Russians will be beaten: this is crazy, you cannot beat the Russians. I beg you to settle upon the frontier question.*' Later in the discussion, when the Polish Prime Minister said he could not agree to give up any of eastern Poland, Churchill exclaimed: '*Unless you accept the frontier you are out of business forever. The Russians will sweep through your country and your people will be liquidated. . . . In your obstinacy you do not see what is at stake. . . . You will start another war in which 25 million lives will be lost.*' When one of the Poles present spoke of the desires of Polish public opinion, Churchill remarked: '*But what is it that your public opinion demands. The right to be crushed?*'

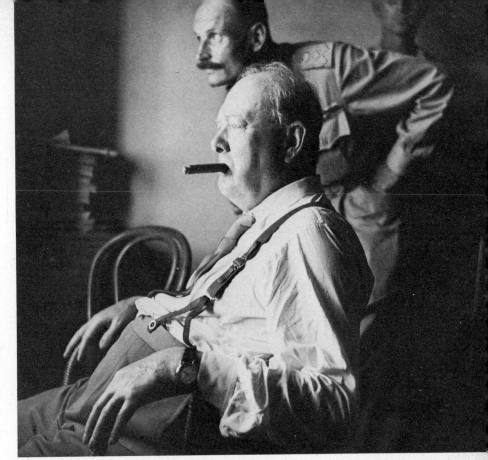

**316
and
317**

During his visit to the
Italian front, Churchill
watched Allied artillery in
action, from a Forward
Observation Post.

318 Paris was liberated from the Germans on 24 August 1944, while Churchill was in Italy. On 10 November he flew to Paris for political discussions with the French leaders, and on the following day he and de Gaulle watched the armistice day parade. Immediately behind Churchill (to his right) is Sir Alexander Cadogan, Permanent Under-Secretary of State for Foreign Affairs, who accompanied Churchill on most of his wartime journeys abroad, and who recorded in his diary that evening: '*Procession, which lasted a full hour, v. good. . . . Enormous, enthusiastic and good-humoured crowd who, most of the time, chanted Chur-chill!*' On 16 November, after he had returned to England, Churchill wrote to de Gaulle: '*I shall always recall as one of the proudest and most moving occasions of my life the wonderful reception which the people of Paris gave to their British guests on this our first visit to your capital after its liberation. I was also most grateful of the opportunity of seeing for myself something of the ardour and high quality of French troops, which are completing the liberation of their native soil. . . .*'

319 Throughout December, the situation in Greece caused Churchill much anxiety. He was much afraid that, with the Germans being driven out, the Greek Communists would seize control. By 17 December, civil war had broken out in Athens itself. On 22 December Churchill wrote to Field Marshal Smuts that '*if the powers of evil prevail in Greece, as is quite likely, we must be prepared for a quasi-Bolshevised Russian-led Balkan peninsula, and this may spread to Italy and Hungary*'. Churchill decided to go to Greece himself, and, abandoning his family Christmas, flew to Athens on 24 December, together with Anthony Eden. On 26 December he met Archbishop Damaskinos (with whom he is seen in this photograph) and persuaded the Archbishop to become Regent of Greece. To his wife, Churchill telegraphed on 26 December: '*The Conference at Greek Foreign Office was intensely dramatic. All those haggard Greek faces around the table, and the Archbishop with his enormous hat, making him, I should think, seven feet tall. . . . We have now left them together, as it was a Greek show. It may break up at any moment. At least we have done our best.*'

320

On 29 December Churchill returned from Athens to London; a month later, on 29 January he left London for the Soviet town of Yalta, in the Crimea, and for seven days, beginning on 4 February, discussed the future of Germany, of Poland, and of Eastern Europe, with Stalin and Roosevelt. On 8 February Churchill told the Conference: '*Do not let us underestimate the difficulties. Nations, comrades in arms, have in the past drifted apart within five or ten years of war. Thus toiling millions have followed a vicious circle, falling into the pit, and then by their sacrifices raising themselves up again. We now have a chance of avoiding the errors of previous generations and of making a sure peace. People cry out for peace and joy. Will the families be reunited? Will the warrior come home? Will the shattered dwellings be rebuilt? Will the toiler see his home? To defend one's country is glorious, but there are greater conquests before us. Before us lies the realisation of the dream of the poor—that they shall live in peace, protected by our invincible power from aggression and evil.*' This photograph shows Churchill and Roosevelt in private conclave at Yalta.

**321
and
322**   Churchill and Stalin arriving for one of the Yalta banquets.

323 Stalin and Churchill at Yalta. Proposing a toast to Stalin at dinner on 8 February 1945, Churchill said: '*I hope to see the future of Russia bright, prosperous, and happy. I will do anything to help, and I am sure so will the President. There was a time when the Marshal was not so kindly towards us, and I remember that I said a few rude things about him, but our common dangers and common loyalties have wiped all that out. The fire of war has burnt up the misunderstandings of the past. We feel we have a friend whom we can trust, and I hope he will continue to feel the same about us. I pray he may live to see his beloved Russia not only glorious in war, but also happy in peace.*'

324 'The Big Three' at Yalta. Roosevelt, who was already extremely ill, died two months later, on 12 April 1945. Five days later Churchill told the House of Commons: '. . . *at Yalta I noticed that the President was ailing. His captivating smile, his gay and charming manner, had not deserted him, but his face had a transparency, an air of purification, and often there was a far-away look in his eyes. When I took my leave of him in Alexandria harbour I must confess that I had an indefinable sense of fear that his health and his strength were on the ebb. But nothing altered his inflexible sense of duty. To the end he faced his innumerable tasks unflinching. . . . When death came suddenly upon him he had "finished his mail". That portion of his day's work was done. As the saying goes, he died in harness, and we may well say in battle harness, like his soldiers, sailors, and airmen, who side by side with ours are carrying on their task to the end all over the world. What an enviable death was his! He had brought his country through the worst of its perils and the heaviest of its toils. Victory had cast its sure and steady beam upon him. In the days of peace he had broadened and stabilised the foundations of American life and union. In war he had raised the strength, might, and glory of the great Republic to a height never attained by any nation in history.*'

325
and
326
On 7 March 1945, after six weeks of fierce and uninterrupted battles, the American First Army reached, and crossed, the Rhine. Two days later Churchill telegraphed to General Eisenhower: '*No one who studies war can fail to be inspired by the admirable speed and flexibility of the American armies . . . and the adaptiveness of commanders and their troops to the swiftly changing conditions of modern battles on the greatest scale.*' In mid-March General Montgomery planned to cross the upper Rhine with 80,000 Allied troops, and break into the industrial Ruhr. Churchill flew from London to Venlo, on the Meuse, on 23 March, in order to be in the battle zone at the time of the attack. The river was crossed at several points during 24 March, and Churchill throughout the day watched the attacks. These two photographs show him riding in an American armoured car on the western bank of the Rhine, and in the German town of Xanten.

327 Looking across the Rhine, 25 March 1945.

328 On board a United States landing craft, crossing the Rhine, 25 March 1945.

On 25 March 1945 Churchill and Montgomery went to see Eisenhower farther south. Churchill recorded in his memoirs: *'The Rhine – here about four hundred yards broad – flowed at our feet. There was a smooth, flat expanse of meadows on the enemy's side. The officers told us that the far bank was unoccupied so far as they knew, and we gazed and gaped at it for a while. . . . Then the Supreme Commander had to depart on other business, and Montgomery and I were about to follow his example when I saw a small launch come close by to moor. So I said to Montgomery, "Why don't we go across and have a look at the other side?" Somewhat to my surprise he answered, "Why not?" After he had made some inquiries we started across the river with three or four American commanders and half a dozen armed men. We landed in brilliant sunshine and perfect peace on the German shore, and walked about for half an hour or so unmolested.'*

329 Landing on the eastern bank of the Rhine, 25 March 1945.

330 Churchill on the Wesel bridge. After crossing back to the western bank of the Rhine on 25 March, Montgomery had suggested to Churchill that they visit the railway bridge at Wesel, where some action was still in progress. In his memoirs Churchill recalled: '*So we got into his car, and, accompanied by the Americans, who were delighted at the prospect, we went to the big iron-girder railway bridge, which was broken in the middle but whose twisted ironwork offered good perches. The Germans were replying to our fire, and their shells fell in salvos of four about a mile away. Presently they came nearer. Then one salvo came overhead and plunged in the water on our side of the bridge. The shells seemed to explode on impact with the bottom, and raised great fountains of spray about a hundred yards away. Several other shells fell among the motor-cars which were concealed not far behind us, and it was decided we ought to depart. I clambered down and joined my adventurous host for our two hours' drive back to his headquarters.*'

331 Churchill, General Brooke, and General Montgomery, picnic on the bank of the Rhine, 26 March 1945. Churchill has thrust his walking stick into the ground; it had been given to him as a wedding present in 1908 by King Edward VII.

332 Clement Attlee and Churchill leave Westminster Abbey, after the memorial service to Lloyd George, 11 April 1945. Lloyd George had died on 26 March 1945; two days later Churchill told the House of Commons: *'There was no man so gifted, so eloquent, so forceful, who knew the life of the people so well. His warm heart was stirred by the many perils which beset the cottage homes: the health of the bread-winner, the fate of his widow, the nourishment and upbringing of his children, the meagre and haphazard provision of medical treatment and sanatoria, and the lack of any organized accessible medical service of a kind worthy of the age, from which the mass of the wage earners and the poor suffered. All this excited his wrath. Pity and compassion lent their powerful wings. He knew the terror with which old age threatened the toiler – that after a life of exertion he could be no more than a burden at the fireside and in the family of a struggling son. When I first became Lloyd George's friend and active associate, now more than forty years ago, this deep love of the people, the profound knowledge of their lives and of the undue and needless pressures under which they lived, impressed itself indelibly upon my mind.'*

334 At three o'clock on the afternoon of 8 May, Churchill broadcast to the nation from 10 Downing Street. During the course of his speech he said: *'Today, perhaps, we shall think mostly of ourselves. To-morrow we shall pay a particular tribute to our Russian comrades, whose prowess in the field has been one of the grand contributions to the general victory. . . . We may allow ourselves a brief period of rejoicing; but let us not forget for a moment the toil and efforts that lie ahead. Japan, with all her treachery and greed, remains unsubdued. The injury she has inflicted on Great Britain, the United States, and other countries, and her detestable cruelties, call for justice and retribution. We must now devote all our strength and resources to the completion of our task, both at home and abroad. Advance, Britannia. Long live the cause of freedom. God save the King.'*

333

The German forces in Europe surrendered to the Allies on 7 May 1945. On the following day victory celebrations were held throughout Britain. This photograph shows Churchill on his way to the House of Commons, surrounded by an exhilarated crowd. A few minutes earlier, from the balcony of the Ministry of Health, he had declared: *'God bless you all. This is your victory. It is the victory of the cause of freedom in every land. In all our long history we have never seen a greater day than this. Everyone, man or woman, has done their best. Everyone has tried. Neither the long years, nor the dangers, nor the fierce attacks of the enemy, have in any way weakened the independent resolve of the British nation. God bless you all.'*

335 and 336   With the end of the war in Europe, the Labour Party insisted upon an end to the Coalition, and a return to Party politics. On 4 June 1945 Churchill made his first election broadcast. Speaking as Leader of the Conservative Party, he declared: '*My friends, I must tell you that a Socialist policy is abhorrent to the British ideas of freedom. Although it is now put forward in the main by people who have a good grounding in the Liberalism and Radicalism of the early part of this century, there can be no doubt that Socialism is inseparably interwoven with Totalitarianism and the abject worship of the State. It is not alone that property, in all its forms, is struck at, but that liberty, in all its forms, is challenged by the fundamental conceptions of Socialism. . . . No Socialist Government conducting the entire life and industry of the country could afford to allow free, sharp, or violently-worded expressions of public discontent. They would have to fall back on some form of Gestapo, no doubt very humanely directed in the first instance. And this would nip opinion in the bud; it would stop criticism as it reared its head, and it would gather all the power to the supreme party and the party leaders, rising like stately pinnacles above their vast bureaucracies of Civil servants, no longer servants and no longer civil. And where would the ordinary people simple folk – the common people, as they like to call them in America – where would they be, once this mighty organism had got them in its grip?*' This was Churchill's principal theme throughout the campaign; here he is seen speaking in public. With him in the car is Captain Margesson (a former Conservative Party Chief Whip).

337 Churchill and his wife touring Churchill's own constituency, Woodford, 26 May 1945. In his fourth and last, election broadcast, on 30 June, he said: '*This is the last of the broadcasts of this election. It ends the series which the B.B.C. have placed at the disposal of the politicians, and it may be the last time that I shall so address you through this medium as Prime Minister. That rests with you. I am convinced that I can help you through the dangers and difficulties of the next few years with more advantage than would fall to others, and I am ready, if desired, to try my best. I await your answer. It must be Aye or No. I await it not with pride or thirst for power – for what have I to gain or lose after all that has happened, and all you have done for me? But I await your answer with confidence. I have high confidence in the answer you will give.*'

338

Churchill addressing an audience of 20,000 people at Walthamstow, 4 July 1945. Three days later he left for a short holiday in the South of France. The election results would not be known until 26 July, as the votes of soldiers serving abroad had all to be counted.

339 On 15 July 1945 Churchill flew to Berlin for a final conference with Stalin at Potsdam. In this photograph he is shown shaking hands with the new President of the United States, Harry S. Truman. It was the first time they had met since Truman had become President. *'I called on him the morning after our arrival'*, Churchill later wrote, *'and was impressed with his gay, precise, sparkling manner and obvious power of decision.'*

340 Visiting the ruins of Hitler's Chancellery, Berlin, 16 July 1945. Churchill's daughter Mary is at his side; his conference interpreter, Major Birse (who translated for him in his discussions with Stalin) is on his left (in military uniform, with jacket). '*In the square in front of the Chancellery . . .*' Churchill wrote in his memoirs, '*except for one old man who shook his head disapprovingly, they all began to cheer. My hate had died with their surrender. . . .*'

341 Leaving Hitler's underground bunker, Berlin, 16 July 1945. '*I went down to the bottom*', Churchill later recalled, '*and saw the room in which he and his mistress had committed suicide, and when we came up again they showed us the place where his body had been burned.*'

342 On 21 July 1945 Churchill took the salute at a Victory Parade in Berlin. Among those in the parade were troops of the 7th Armoured Division – 'The Desert Rats' – to whom Churchill spoke later that day, at the opening of the 'Winston Club' for British troops in Berlin. During his speech he said: *'This morning's parade brings back to my mind a great many moving incidents of these last long fierce years. Now you are here in Berlin, and I find you established in this great centre which, as a volcano, erupted smoke and fire all over Europe. Twice in our generation as in bygone times the German fury has been unleashed on her neighbours. . . . Now it is we who take our place in the occupation of this country. . . . I am unable to speak without emotion. Dear Desert Rats, may your glory ever shine. May your laurels never fade. May the memory of this glorious pilgrimage which you have made from Alamein to the Baltic and Berlin never die. A march – as far as my reading of history leads me to believe – unsurpassed in the whole story of war. May fathers long tell their children the tale. May you all feel that through following your great ancestors you have accomplished something which has done good to the whole world, which has raised the honour of your country and of which every man has the right to feel proud.'*

343 The saluting base. From left to right: Lord Cherwell (Churchill's scientific adviser and wartime confidant); Montgomery; Sir Alexander Cadogan (forehead only); Churchill; General Ismay (Churchill's personal military secretary and adviser), Field Marshal Alexander and, paper in hand, Churchill's doctor, Lord Moran.

344

Churchill left the Potsdam negotiations in mid-course, and returned to London to learn the results of the 1945 election, which were announced on 26 July. Labour won 393 seats, the Conservatives only 213. That night Churchill went to Buckingham Palace and resigned his position as Prime Minister. This photograph shows him on the way to the Palace. He was succeeded as Prime Minister by Clement Attlee. That same night, Sir Alexander Cadogan wrote in a private letter from Potsdam: *'The election will have come as a terrible blow to poor old Winston, and I am awfully sorry for the old boy. It certainly is a display of base ingratitude, and rather humiliating for our country.'* Churchill himself wrote to Cadogan on 5 August that the Labour victory would *'diminish our national stature at a time when we most need unity and strength'*.

345

In 1946 Churchill went to the United States, where he was again welcomed with enthusiasm and received a host of honorary degrees from universities throughout the country. On 5 March 1946 he was at Westminster College, Fulton, Missouri, where he was introduced to the audience by President Truman. In a solemn speech, he warned of the twin dangers of War and Tyranny, spoke of the 'Iron Curtain' which had descended across Europe, and argued forcefully in favour of a 'special relationship' between Britain and the United States. During the course of his speech he declared: *'I repulse the idea that a new war is inevitable, still more that it is imminent. . . . I do not believe that Soviet Russia desires war. What they desire is the fruits of war and the indefinite expansion of their power and doctrines. But what we have to consider here to-day while time remains, is the permanent prevention of war and the establishment of conditions of freedom and democracy as rapidly as possible in all countries. . . .*

On 8 March Churchill went to Richmond, Virginia – he is seen here arriving at the station, followed by General Eisenhower, Mrs Churchill and Mrs Eisenhower. In his speech to the General Assembly of Virginia he said: *'Peace will not be preserved by pious sentiment, expressed in terms of platitudes or by official grimaces and diplomatic correctitude, however desirable this may be from time to time. It will not be preserved by casting aside in dangerous years the panoply of warlike strength. There must be earnest thought. There must also be faithful perseverance and foresight. Greatheart must have his sword and armour to guard the pilgrims on their way. Above all, among the English-speaking peoples, there must be the union of hearts based upon conviction and common ideals. That is what I offer. That is what I seek.'*

347 Flying home from Marrakesh.

346
Throughout 1946 and 1947 Churchill was at work on his war memoirs, the first volume of which, 'The Gathering Storm', was published in 1948. At the end of 1947 he suffered from a severe attack of bronchitis, and went to Morocco to recuperate. Here he is seen painting, in Marrakesh, on 18 January 1948.

348

A persistent theme of Churchill's speeches while he was Leader of the Opposition (from 1945 to 1951) was the unity of Europe. On 7 May 1948 he told the Congress of Europe at the Hague: '*A high and a solemn responsibility rests upon us here this afternoon in this Congress of a Europe striving to be reborn. If we allow ourselves to be rent and disordered by pettiness and small disputes, if we fail in clarity of view or courage in action, a priceless occasion may be cast away for ever. But if we all pull together and pool the luck and the comradeship – and we shall need all the comradeship and not a little luck if we are to move together in this way – and firmly grasp the larger hopes of humanity, then it may be that we shall move into a happier sunlit age, when all the little children who are now growing up in this tormented world may find themselves not the victors nor the vanquished in the fleeting triumphs of one country over another in the bloody turmoil of destructive war, but the heirs of all the treasures of the past and the masters of all the science, the abundance and the glories of the future.*' This photograph shows Churchill at the end of his speech, overwhelmed by the response. From left to right are four of the leaders of the European movement: Dr Kerstens (Holland), Paul Ramadier (France), Dr Retinger (Secretary General of the Congress) and Denis de Rougemont.

349

An indefatigable speaker, Churchill led the Conservative attack on the Labour Government in the House of Commons, and spoke throughout Britain. This photograph was taken in Cambridge in June 1948. A month later, on 10 July, he told his constituents: '*Never under a socialist Government or while they follow the lines of Socialist restriction, wrong planning, wasteful management, and administrative incompetence will this country regain its sovereignty and independence.*'

351

At the General Election of 1950, the Labour Party was again returned to power, but with a majority of only five seats over all other parties. Another General Election was held on 25 October 1951. Here Churchill is seen going to cast his vote. The Conservatives were re-elected to power by a majority of only 17, and with less overall votes than Labour. Churchill became Prime Minister for the second time, holding office until 1955.

350

Churchill at Chartwell, 1950. It was at Chartwell that he painted, prepared his speeches, and finished his six-volume war memoirs, 'The Second World War'.

352 On 7 January 1953 Churchill visited Bermuda. Here he is seen leaving the aeroplane with his son-in-law, Christopher Soames, and his Principal Private Secretary, J. R. Colville. He had flown from the United States in President Eisenhower's personal aircraft.

353 On 14 June 1954 Churchill was installed at Windsor Castle as a Knight of the Garter, becoming 'Sir' Winston. But he later refused the Queen's offer of a Dukedom, not wanting to leave the House of Commons, or to lose the name 'Churchill'.

354 In June 1954 Churchill went to the United States for further talks with President Dwight D. Eisenhower. With Churchill and Eisenhower is the Vice-President, Richard M. Nixon. A year earlier, in June 1953, he had suffered a severe stroke, and had been unable for some time to attend to public affairs.

355

As Prime Minister from 1951 to 1955, Churchill remained a supporter of European unity. But the comprehensive unity of which he had spoken in the late 1940's proved impossible to secure in the early 1950's. Here he is at Chartwell on 23 August 1954, with the French Prime Minister, Pierre Mendès-France, after they had held emergency discussions on the breakdown of the European Defence Committee Conference at Brussels.

356 In March 1955 Churchill decided to resign, and on 4 April 1955, his last night as Prime Minister, he gave a dinner at 10 Downing Street for the Queen and Prince Philip. This photograph was taken as his guests left. Two days later, on 6 April 1955, he himself left 10 Downing Street.

357

Churchill at Chartwell; a photograph taken on 30 November 1955, his eighty-first birthday While in retirement, he worked on a four-volume 'History of the English Speaking Peoples' which he had begun in the late 1930's, and which was published between 1956 and 1958 The book won him the Nobel Prize for Literature.

358 Relaxing at Roquebrune, in the South of France, with Field-Marshal Viscount Montgomery, 12 October 1957.

359 Churchill on his Golden Wedding Anniversary, 12 September 1958. With him are his son Randolph, Lady Churchill, and Randolph Churchill's daughter Arabella. This photograph was taken at The Villa Capponcina, Lord Beaverbrook's house on the Cap d'Ail, Nice.

360 Churchill painting in the South of France. For the last years of his life, painting was his principal relaxation.

361

While sailing as a guest on Aristotle Onassis' yacht 'Christina' in September 1960, Churchill was the guest of the Yugoslav leader, Marshal Tito, and landed briefly on Yugoslav soil.

362 Playing bezique at Chartwell in 1964, with the Hon. Mrs Anthony Henley, a close family friend.

363 Relaxing in a garden in the South of France.

Churchill died at his London home on 25 January 1965, at the age of ninety. After the lying in State at Westminster Hall, the funeral service was held at St Paul's Cathedral on 30 January. The funeral procession was watched by thousands of people in the streets of London, and by millions on television. Several years before, with typical foresight and thoroughness, Churchill himself had laid down in precise detail how the procession was to be made up – what route it was to take, which tunes the bands were to play, and which hymns were to be sung; and he had given this last great plan of action the code-name: *'Operation Hope Not'*.

364 Churchill's coffin being taken from St Paul's to Waterloo Station, as part of the final journey to Bladon churchyard near Blenheim Palace, where he was buried next to his father, mother, and brother.

List of Sources for the Photographs

1 Churchill Photograph Albums: Broadwater collection
2 Churchill Biography: Photographic collection
3 Churchill Photograph Albums: Broadwater collection
4 Churchill Photograph Albums: Broadwater collection
5 Churchill Biography: Photographic collection
6 Radio Times Hulton Picture Library: P 240
7 Radio Times Hulton Picture Library: P 600
8 Churchill Biography: Photographic collection
9 Churchill Photograph Albums: Broadwater collection
10 Churchill Photograph Albums: Broadwater collection
11 Churchill Photograph Albums: Broadwater collection
12 Churchill Biography: Photographic collection
13 Churchill Photograph Albums: Broadwater collection
14 Churchill Photograph Albums: Broadwater collection
15 Churchill Press Cutting Albums: *Illustrated Sporting and Dramatic News*, 25 November 1899
16 Longmans, Publishers
17 Churchill Photograph Albums: Broadwater collection
18 Radio Times Hulton Picture Library: 15291
19 Churchill Biography: Photographic collection
20 Churchill Press Cutting Albums: *The Saturday Herald*, 18 November 1899
21 Churchill Press Cutting Albums: *Daily News Weekly*, 25 November 1899
22 Edition Nels, Brussels
23 Churchill Press Cutting Albums: Pasted-in photograph
24 Churchill Press Cutting Albums: *Police News*, 6 January 1900
25 Churchill Photograph Albums: Broadwater collection
26 Churchill Photograph Albums: Broadwater collection
27 Churchill Photograph Albums: Broadwater collection
28 Churchill Photograph Albums: Broadwater collection
29 Churchill Photograph Albums: Broadwater collection
30 J. Bowers, Pretoria (provided by J. R. A. Bailey, Johannesburg)
31 Longmans, Publishers
32 Spy cartoon, Vanity Fair, 10 July 1900
33 Churchill Photograph Albums: Broadwater collection
34 Cardiff Naturalists Society
35 Churchill Photograph Albums: Broadwater collection
36 Churchill Press Cutting Albums: *Punch*, 10 September 1902
37 Churchill Photograph Albums: Broadwater collection
38 Therize Borry (provided by Paul Maze)
39 Radio Times Hulton Picture Library: P 4954
40 Churchill Press Cutting Albums: *Manchester Daily Despatch*, 19 March 1904
41 Churchill Press Cutting Albums: *Pall Mall Gazette*, 7 June 1904
42 Radio Times Hulton Picture Library: P 24523
43 Radio Times Hulton Picture Library: P 15777

44–50 Churchill Press Cutting Albums: original photographs by R. Banks
51 Churchill Photograph Albums: Broadwater collection
52 Churchill Papers: Chartwell Trust collection
53 Churchill Photograph Albums: Broadwater collection
54 Churchill Papers: Chartwell Trust collection
55 Churchill Papers: Chartwell Trust collection
56 Daily Mirror Picture Service
57 Churchill Press Cutting Albums: *Daily Mirror*, 11 May 1908
58 Bassano & Vandyk: G/B85A
59 Syndication International: DM 778 K
60 Churchill Photograph Album: Broadwater collection
61 Churchill Biography: Photographic collection
62 Die Woche (cutting sent by Mr and Mrs H Sornsen)
63 Barratt's Photo Press: P 71973
64 Churchill Press Cutting Albums: *Black & White*, 11 December 1909
65 Radio Times Hulton Picture Library: P 18993
66 Radio Times Hulton Picture Library: P 2547
67 Churchill Biography: Photographic collection
68 Churchill Photograph Albums: Broadwater collection
69 Churchill Press Cutting Albums: *Illustrated London News*, 10 April 1909
70 Churchill Press Cutting Albums: *Manchester Evening News*, 16 November 1909
71 Sport and General Press Agency: G 1408/13
72 Press Association: A 1738
73 Press Association: A 1286
74 Mrs Eva Reichmann (original at Blenheim Palace)
75 Radio Times Hulton Picture Library: P 15784
76 E. T. Reed
77 Baroness Spencer-Churchill photograph album
78 Churchill Biography: Photographic collection
79 Press Association: B 1214
80 Churchill Biography: Photographic collection
81 Press Association: A 1886
82 Press Association: B 1203
83 Radio Times Hulton Picture Library: P 13529
84 Radio Times Hulton Picture Library: P 16261
85 Churchill Photograph Albums: Broadwater collection
86 Chartwell Trust Papers; photograph by Campbell Gray: A 424
87 Radio Times Hulton Picture Library: P 2443
88 Churchill Press Cutting Albums: *Dover Express*, 27 April 1912
89 Press Association: C 1205
90 Press Association: C 1200
91 Radio Times Hulton Picture Library: P 15528
92 Radio Times Hulton Picture Library: P 15482
93 Radio Times Hulton Picture Library: P 13481
94 Mrs Constance Mainprice (photograph taken by Fleet Paymaster E. L. Mainprice)
95 Churchill Press Cutting Albums: *The Bystander*, 4 June 1913
96 Churchill Press Cutting Albums: *Punch*, 21 May 1913
97 Radio Times Hulton Picture Library: P 15765

98 Press Association: G 1204
99 Press Association: E 1327
100 Press Association: D 1237
101 Sport and General: 9261
102 Churchill Press Cutting Albums: *Ulk*, no 48, Berlin, 28 November 1913
103 Churchill Press Cutting Albums: *Birmingham Evening Despatch*, 1 December 1913
104 Churchill Photograph Albums: Broadwater collection
105 Churchill Photograph Albums: Broadwater collection
106 Radio Times Hulton Picture Library: P 15525
107 Churchill Press Cutting Albums: *The Bystander*, 28 January 1914
108 Radio Times Hulton Picture Library: Y 36686
109 Press Association: E 1218
110 Press Association: B 1207
111 Lady Patricia Kingsbury
112 Churchill Press Cutting Albums: *Punch*, 25 May 1914
113 Radio Times Hulton Picture Library: P 2444
114 Press Association: E 1207
115 Poy, 4 August 1914
116 Churchill Press Cutting Albums: *The Tatler*, 12 August 1914
117 Churchill Press Cutting Albums: *Everyman*, 21 August 1914
118 Churchill Press Cutting Albums: *Great Deeds of the War*, 12 December 1914
119 Syndication International: FF10
120 Peregrine S. Churchill
121 Poy, 30 November 1915
122 Press Association: F 1249
123 Harry Skinner
124 Churchill Press Cutting Albums: *Manchester Dispatch*, 19 February 1915
125 Churchill Press Cutting Albums: *Westminster Gazette*, 25 February 1915
126 Imperial War Museum: Q 13619
127 Radio Times Hulton Picture Library: 062913-P
128 Radio Times Hulton Picture Library: 062912-P
129 Churchill Press Cutting Albums: *The Bystander*, 2 June 1915
130 Imperial War Museum: Q 11428
131 London News Agency
132 Press Association: G 1351
133 Press Association: F 1217
134 Press Association: F 1218
135 Press Association: G 1244
136 Press Association: G 1245
137 Radio Times Hulton Picture Library: P 15774
138 Churchill Photograph Albums: Broadwater collection
139 Churchill Biography: Photographic collection
140 Major-General Sir Edmund Hakewill-Smith
141 European Picture Service
142 Chartwell Trust Papers: *London Magazine*, October 1916 (photograph by Dinham, Torquay)
143 Radio Times Hulton Picture Library: P 15782
144 Radio Times Hulton Picture Library: P 21862

145 Radio Times Hulton Picture Library: P 22055
146 Imperial War Museum: Q 11428
147 Associated Newspapers
148 Churchill Press Cutting Albums: *The Star*, 21 January 1920
149 Churchill Photograph Albums: Broadwater collection
150 Churchill Photograph Albums: Broadwater collection
151 K. C. Felce
152 Press Association: K 48
153 Radio Times Hulton Picture Library: 14112-P
154 Press Association: K 1304
155 Trenchard Photograph Albums
156 Churchill Photograph Albums: Broadwater collection
157 Churchill Photograph Albums: Broadwater collection
158 Churchill Photograph Albums: Broadwater collection
159 Press Association: N 1226
160 Churchill Photograph Albums: Broadwater collection
161 Press Association: P 1288
162 Syndication International: DM 799 T
163 Churchill Press Cutting Albums: *The Weekly Westminster*, 15 March 1924
164 Press Association: 102168–62
165 Press Association: 102168–15
166 Churchill Press Cutting Albums: *Punch*, 4 June 1924
167 Churchill Press Cutting Albums: *The Star*, 7 October 1924
168 Churchill Photograph Albums: Broadwater collection
169 Central Press Photos: Box 1525/1
170 Syndication International: DM 780 F
171 Syndication International: DM 780 G
172 Churchill Photograph Albums: Broadwater collection
173 Churchill Photograph Albums: Broadwater collection
174 Syndication International: DM 760 L
175 Associated Press: B 12811
176 Churchill Photograph Albums: Broadwater collection
177 Topical Press Agency: D 7630
178 Churchill Photograph Albums: Broadwater collection
179 Churchill Photograph Albums: Broadwater collection
180 Churchill Photograph Albums: Broadwater collection
181 Churchill Photograph Albums: Broadwater collection
182 Churchill Photograph Albums: Broadwater collection
183 Radio Times Hulton Picture Library: E 358P-P
184 Radio Times Hulton Picture Library: E 7361-P
185 Radio Times Hulton Picture Library: E 8410-P
186 United Press International, Planet News: LN 5210
187 Martin Gilbert Archive
188 Press Association: U 1203
189 Churchill Photograph Albums: Broadwater collection
190 Churchill Photograph Albums: Broadwater collection
191 Churchill Photograph Albums: Broadwater collection
192 Associated Press: 29740

193 Press Association: V 1384
194 Syndication International: DM 7807
195 Churchill Photograph Albums: Broadwater collection
196 Radio Times Hulton Picture Library: G 8535-P
197 Radio Times Hulton Picture Library: G 9496-P
198 Associated Press: 50307
199 Press Association: X 1215
200 Churchill Press Cutting Albums: *Daily Herald*, 30 March 1933
201 Associated Press: 106927
202 Syndication International: OP 708 E
203 Radio Times Hulton Picture Library: 54374 P
204 Ava, Viscountess Waverley
205 Ava, Viscountess Waverley
206 Radio Times Hulton Picture Library: P 239
207 Radio Times Hulton Picture Library: T 2899 P
208 Topix (Thomson Newspapers)
209 Associated Press: 192483
210 Radio Times Hulton Picture Library: P 5012
211 Radio Times Hulton Picture Library: P 241
212 Radio Times Hulton Picture Library: P 5779
213 Radio Times Hulton Picture Library: P 53031
214 Fox Photos: 218803
215 Radio Times Hulton Picture Library: V 2356-P
216 Associated Press: 208468
217 Churchill Press Cutting Albums: *Punch*, 31 May 1939
218 Churchill Press Cutting Albums: *Daily Express*, 6 July 1939
219 Churchill Press Cutting Albums: *Punch*, 12 July 1939
220 *Daily Mirror*, 25 July 1939
221 Paul Maze
222 Paul Maze
223 Associated Press: 214842
224 Churchill Press Cutting Albums: *The Tatler*, 6 September 1939
225 United Press International: 88814
226 Associated Press: 215679
227 Associated Press: 216223
228 Fox Photos: HP 46253
229 Radio Times Hulton Picture Library: V 6124-P
230 Churchill Press Cutting Albums: no newspaper source given
231 Imperial War Museum: O 190
232 Imperial War Museum: O 188
233 *Simplicissimus* (Munich), 5 November 1939
234 Syndication International: OP 708-F
235 Churchill Press Cutting Albums: *Evening Standard*, 13 November 1939
236 Sir Geoffrey Shakespeare
237 Central Press Photos: Box 5233
238 Radio Times Hulton Picture Library: W 720 P
239 Radio Times Hulton Picture Library: W 882 P
240 Associated Press: 223945

241   Associated Press: 224159
242   Radio Times Hulton Picture Library: W 2360 P
243   Radio Times Hulton Picture Library: W 2418 P
244   Radio Times Hulton Picture Library: W 2418 A-P
245   Associated Press: 225376
246   Churchill Press Cutting Albums: *Daily Mail*, 13 May 1940
247   Associated Press: 225592
248   Sir Cecil Beaton
249   Radio Times Hulton Picture Library: W 2628 P
250   Baroness Spencer-Churchill photograph album
251   Imperial War Museum: H 3516
252   Imperial War Museum: H 3504
253   Imperial War Museum: H 3977
254   Fox Photos: WE 1216
255   Central Press Photos
256   Associated Press: 230388
257   George Rance
258   George Rance
259   Radio Times Hulton Picture Library: W 5547 P
260   Radio Times Hulton Picture Library: W 5548 P
261   Radio Times Hulton Picture Library: W 5549 P
262   Acme News Pictures
263   Churchill Biography: Photographic collection
264   United Press International
265   Radio Times Hulton Picture Library: Y 1851 P
266   Radio Times Hulton Picture Library: Y 1855 P
267   Radio Times Hulton Picture Library: Y 1857 P
268   Radio Times Hulton Picture Library: Y 1858A P
269   Czechoslovak Army Film & Photo Service: No 38
270   Czechoslovak Army Film & Photo Service: No 33
271   Czechoslovak Army Film & Photo Service: No 48
272   Churchill Photograph Albums: Broadwater collection
273   Churchill Photograph Albums: Broadwater collection
274   Churchill Photograph Albums: Broadwater collection
275   Churchill Photograph Albums: Broadwater collection
276   Churchill Photograph Albums: Broadwater collection
277   A. Massen
278   Imperial War Museum: H 14201
279   Imperial War Museum: H 14266
280   Imperial War Museum: H 14259
281   Radio Times Hulton Picture Library: Y 2628 P
282   Camera Press: 7016–2
283   Winston S. Churchill MP: Private collection
284   Churchill Photograph Albums: Broadwater collection
285   Churchill Photograph Albums: Broadwater collection
286   Churchill Photograph Albums: Broadwater collection
287   Churchill Photograph Albums: Broadwater collection
288   Churchill Photograph Albums: Broadwater collection

337 Press Association: 102168–32
338 Central Press Photos: Box 5414
339 Field Marshal Viscount Montgomery's photograph albums
340 Imperial War Museum: BU 8954
341 Imperial War Museum: BU 8955
342 Field Marshal Earl Alexander of Tunis' photograph albums
343 Field Marshal Earl Alexander of Tunis' photograph albums
344 Associated Press: 280447
345 Charles T. Mayer
346 United Press International
347 Mr Harvey
348 Radio Times Hulton Picture Library: P 1233
349 D. Freeman
350 Time Incorporated and Miss Grace Hamblin
351 United Press International
352 Churchill Photograph Albums: Broadwater collection
353 Baroness Spencer-Churchill photograph album
354 Churchill Biography: Photographic collection
355 United Press International
356 United Press International
357 Vivienne, London; Camera Press 2589–31
358 Field Marshal Viscount Montgomery's photograph albums
359 United Press International
360 Churchill Biography: Photographic collection
361 Churchill papers: Chartwell Trust collection
362 Paris Match: No 825
363 Paul Maze
364 Topix (Thomson Newspapers)

List of Sources for the Quotations

H. H. Asquith papers (photograph numbers: 71, 73, 80, 82, 107, 127, 132, 137); Margot Asquith papers (121); Balfour papers (128, 140); Baruch papers (214); Cabinet papers, Public Record Office (84, 123, 131); Cadogan papers (318, 344); Jack Churchill papers (33, 120, 142); Lord Randolph Churchill papers, Blenheim Palace Archive, (4, 9); Randolph Churchill papers (189); Elgin papers (54); Fisher papers (87); Jellicoe papers (115); T. E. Lawrence papers (51); Leonie Leslie papers (31); Lloyd George papers (106); Londonderry papers (25); Pamela, Countess of Lytton papers (17, 27, 28); Marquess of Milford Haven papers (88); Venetia Montagu papers (119, 121); Mottistone papers (130); Countess Mountbatten of Burma papers (42); Harold Nicolson papers (205); Rosebery papers (36); Royal Archives (73, 75); Spears papers (138); Baroness Spencer-Churchill papers (56, 60, 67, 70, 77, 78, 85, 89, 99, 105, 112, 114, 138, 139, 141, 152, 181, 182); Quickswood papers (39); Ava, Viscountess Waverley papers (203).

All other quotations are from the Churchill papers (Chartwell Trust Collection), or from Churchill's own writings and speeches.

Biographical Index

compiled by the author

I have included only those individuals whom I have been able to identify in the photographs, and have not indexed those that appear in the cartoons, or Churchill himself. Anyone who is identified after the book has been published will be included in both the index and the captions of subsequent editions.